Contents

Preface

Children Can Worship God

Yes, children can worship God . . .
but they must first know who He is.

An Approach to God Illustrated

Junior Church was about to begin for the fourth, fifth, and sixth graders. Suddenly a stranger appeared in the doorway. The leader looked up. "John!" he said, "I'm surprised to see you!"

VISITOR: What's going on here?

LEADER: This is Junior Church.

V: What's that?

L: We worship God.

V: These kids? Whatever do you tell them about God? How do you know there is one?

L: John, don't you believe in God?

V: Oh, I don't know. I've heard different things about God. And I'm not sure what I do believe.

L: Why don't you tell us what you have heard. It would be good for the boys and girls to know what people say.

V: Well, some people say He set the world running, and then left it to itself.

The visitor went on to give another view of God, concluding with the idea that God is power or energy in the universe, not a

7

person. He suggested that this scientific view appealed most to him.

L: John, I'd like to have you know what the Bible says about God. Will you let us tell you?

V: Oh sure. Go ahead.

L: Now, boys and girls, let's tell him what our God is really like.

The children appeared startled, but began to answer. Though most of them had been brought up in the Sunday School, and most had Christian parents, their responses were minimal. The visitor declared that what they told him wasn't enough to impress him.

L: You took us by surprise, John. We leaders have some Bible references about God, but we'd need a few minutes to get them ready for you. Will you stay awhile so we can give you a better answer?

The visitor agreed, and began reading a magazine while he waited. The children quickly gathered in their small groups with their leaders.

How they did dig into their Bibles! For the first time, perhaps, they needed to know who God is and be able to state the biblical facts. Of course, being juniors, many of them had a prior question. "Is that man real? Isn't this a put-up job?"

The leaders calmly replied that the "play" was planned, but added, "You're going to find people in our world who believe that God is just as John described Him. What will you say to them? You didn't have much of an answer."

Even though the children then understood that the situation was not real, they were just as eager to find the Bible information to give to John.

They returned from their groups, and in rapid fire reported to the leader the characteristics of God, which were jotted down on a flip chart with a fiber-tip pen. They had made a list of about 40 characteristics of God,* before the leader turned to John to say, "This is what our God is like." John seemed impressed, said he would think about it, and departed. (Since the visitor was a true

---

* A selected list of characteristics of God from Isaiah is given in the appendix.

8

Christian, he was invited back a couple of weeks later to give his testimony and let the children know that he really was a believer.)

Now the children were invited to choose which characteristics of God on the list they'd especially like to praise God for in their worship services. They promptly chose almost every one!

The leaders were delighted. They selected from the characteristics chosen by the children the ones which seemed easiest for children to understand and appreciate, and arranged them in order, beginning with God as Creator.

For each worship service, one Sunday morning session was spent in preparation. The whole group needed to focus on the characteristic and become appreciative of this facet of God's character. Each small group prepared one part of the service. The following Sunday morning the worship service was held, followed by evaluation in the groups. Then the children made a page for their notebooks to remember the service. They used different handcraft techniques during the course of the months that followed to express their growth in understanding who God is.

In another Junior Church leaders used a different approach to get the characteristics of God before the 9-11 year olds. A woman dressed in Korean national costume was brought to the service as a visitor requesting knowledge of our God. The children reported orally to her after their Bible study, and made a tape recording for her. They unrolled long strips of shelf paper on the floor. Each child was given a space of about a yard, and each drew a picture to show his impression of what God is like. The children chose a Bible story that revealed something about God, or a personal answer to prayer, or an answer to prayer for someone they knew— something which showed that God is real.

Throughout the year the children gained experience in many different ways of worshiping God, by various means of utilizing Scripture, prayer, and music. The following year they chose other characteristics from the list, and their leaders involved them in planning and preparing a service some weeks later.

Evaluation

These two examples illustrate approaches to leading children into real worship experiences by giving them a focus on God.

These illustrations, in turn, provoke many other questions. This book will answer such questions as: What is worship? Who can worship? How can we prepare children for worship? It will also give practical suggestions on how children can worship. You may wish to look up the parts of particular concern to you before you read the whole. But you will need the whole to get a complete perspective.

1

What Is
Worship?

Before we can lead anyone into a worship experience, we must be clear in our thinking.

"I attended church on Sunday." Is that worship?

Is it reading Scripture together? Singing? Giving an offering?

Is it sitting passively while the pastor prays and speaks?

The word *worship* means "worth-ship" and refers to God's worth. It is, therefore, in its highest form, appreciating God for who He is, apart from His works, though we do worship when we express our gratitude to Him for what is tangible. Especially for children, God's abstract characteristics must be tied down to the concrete and to their experiences.

Worship is love, admiration, awe, reverence, adoration. It is "man's heart reaching out to, and communicating with, his Creator." It is "the loving response of an individual's heart to a consciousness of God's presence." It should involve my emotions and my will. I will not worship unless I have a positive attitude toward God. Perhaps these poetic definitions from an old hymnbook will give the feeling which true worship brings:

"Worship is a drop of water in quest of the ocean."

"Worship is the prodigal son running to the Father."

11

"Worship is the lost sheep nestling in the arms of the Rescuer."

A more formal definition says that worship is the "reverent devotion, service, or honor paid to God, whether public or individual" (G. W. Bromiley, "Worship," *The Zondervan Pictorial Encyclopedia of the Bible,* Zondervan, Grand Rapids, Mich.).

Information about God does not necessarily lead into God's presence. Witnessing to the unsaved is not a worship service. A collection of activities on spiritual subjects does not usually lead children to experience worship.

Most adults have not been trained in the art of worship. They are generally inattentive to the words they sing, and to actually praying the pastor's prayer with him. How important then that children learn early to worship "in spirit and in truth." Is it not amazing that our great God is *seeking* such to worship Him? "But an hour is coming, and now is, when the true worshipers shall worship the Father in spirit and truth; for such people the Father seeks to be His worshipers" (John 4:23).

Worship, then, must involve me actively in my inner being.

No one can worship for me. I must meet God face to face myself. And I can. For James tells us to "draw near to God and He will draw near to you" (James 4:8).

The Relationship of Worship and Instruction

The above statement on worship does not describe instruction in the Word, but is vitally related to it. In instruction we learn *about* God; we find out what He says to us, and what we should do. The chief appeal of instruction is to the intellect, the mind. Knowing what the Word says is primary and essential in the Christian life.

Can I recite a list of God's characteristics without loving Him? Yes, I can. Knowing His characteristics is not enough.

I must respond to Him also with my will. "I shall run the way of Thy commandments" (Ps. 119:32). I respond to God's command with action—but only if I love Him and want to please Him.

Good Bible teaching should call for a response in worship, a response of the heart and will. When a person knows what God is like—what He has done and is doing for men—he normally responds to God with love. The first and greatest commandment, according to Jesus, is not to "know the Bible." It is to "love the Lord" with one's whole being.

Man's whole life may be a response to God in loving obedience. "We know that God does not hear sinners; but if anyone is [a worshiper of God], and does His will, He hears him" (John 9:31). But along the way there are moments of decision, moments when a person responds to God's love, and decides to live according to God's will rather than his own. These crucial moments may come in a worship service.

> Thus our aim in planning worship with children
> is to bring them to meet God
> so that they will love Him,
> desire to do His will,
> and determine to do it.

The greatest danger for leaders is to assume that knowing will automatically lead to doing. A careful study of the verbs in Psalm 119, with all its emphasis on the Word of God, produces the amazing discovery that *doing* is mentioned most often ("I will *keep* Thy law continually," v. 44), that *feeling* is next ("I *shall* delight in Thy statutes," v. 16), and that *knowing* the Word is mentioned least often (*"Teach* me Thy statutes," v. 12). This does not mean that knowing is least important, but only that feeling and doing are more difficult and need more attention.

Who can make me worship? No one. Worship is a personal matter, a personal response to God. It is very private. Who knows whether I really do worship? No one but God. What would happen if we were to ask adults at the church door as they departed from the morning worship service, "Did you meet God today in the service?" Probably an open-mouthed silence.

Fortunately we can ask children. We can teach them what worship is. We can set up conditions to help them worship. And we can check up afterward to see if they did meet God. In this way we can learn better how to lead them to worship "with gladness and sincerity of heart," like the believers in the Early Church (Acts 2:46).

Importance of Worship

Is it important to God that I worship? Is it important to me? Scripture answers our questions clearly.

> Tell of His glory among the nations,
> His wonderful deeds among all the peoples.
> For great is the Lord, and greatly to be praised;
> He also is to be feared above all gods.
> For all the gods of the people are idols,
> But the Lord made the heavens.
> Splendor and majesty are before Him,
> Strength and joy are in His place.
>
> Ascribe to the Lord, O families of the peoples,
> Ascribe to the Lord glory and strength.
> Ascribe to the Lord the glory due His name.

See 1 Chronicles 16:8-36 for the rest of this great psalm of praise.

Beginning in Genesis we have examples of worship by those who were in line with God's will. Abraham's servant "bowed low and worshiped the Lord. And he said, 'Blessed be the Lord, the God of my master Abraham, who has not forsaken His loving-kindness and His truth toward my master" (Gen. 24:26-27).

When the people in Egypt "heard that the Lord was concerned about the sons of Israel and that He had seen their affliction, then they bowed low and worshiped" (Ex. 4:31).

When God proclaimed to Moses who He was, "Moses made haste to bow low toward the earth and worship" (Ex. 34:8).

Though David's baby died, he went "into the house of the Lord and worshiped" (2 Sam. 12:20).

When he had lost everything, Job fell to the ground and worshiped (Job 1:20).

When David dedicated the materials for the temple, it was an occasion of great worship (1 Chron. 29). His prayer reflects his knowledge of God's character, but even more his love for God is shown in his gracious willingness to do God's will by allowing Solomon to build the temple. "And all the assembly blessed the Lord, the God of their fathers, and bowed low and [worshiped] the Lord" (29:20).

The New Testament, too, is full of worship, from the wise men's worship of the young Jesus (Matt. 2:11), to the angel's reproof to John, "Worship God" (Rev. 22:9). Many people worshiped the Lord Jesus as He moved among them and they saw His miracles. In heaven also the elders are singing God's praises, and the redeemed throng are singing the worship song of Moses and of the Lamb (Rev. 13:3-4):

Great and marvelous are Thy works,
O Lord God, the Almighty;
Righteous and true are Thy ways,
Thou King of the nations.
Who will not fear, O Lord, and glorify Thy name?
For Thou alone art holy;
For all the nations will come and worship before Thee,
For Thy righteous acts have been revealed.

The Psalms frequently call us to worship: "Let us worship and bow down; let us kneel before the Lord our Maker" (Ps. 95:6); "O Magnify the Lord with me, and let us exalt His name together" (34:3).

Moses (and Jesus' quotation of him—Matthew 4:10)

sounds as if we are being commanded to worship: "You shall set it down before the Lord your God, and worship before the Lord your God; and you . . . shall rejoice in all the good which the Lord your God has given to you and your household" (Deut. 26:10).

Why does God want us to worship Him? Is it for His sake or ours? C. S. Lewis points out that though we may not be able to discern what praise does for God, it reveals our values very clearly. The only *appropriate* response to God is admiration, awe, reverence, worship. "All enjoyment spontaneously overflows into praise" unless checked, and "praise almost seems to be inner health made audible" (*Reflections on the Psalms,* Harcourt, Brace and Company, N.Y.). People praise what they value, and they urge others to join them. Our delights seem to crave expression and sharing.

John Lawing has said it strongly and well:

So here it is, the truest thing I know: Jesus is Lord.

The second truest thing I know is that Lordship is accepted only through worship.

Evangelicals have always seemed to say that what a man believes determines who and what he is. Not so!

It's what a man bows his knees to that determines who he is. It's who or what he acknowledges as Lord that decides it all. That's why the first commandment, "Thou shalt have no other gods before Me," is not a call to belief but a call to worship (*Christianity Today,* Dec. 21, 1973).

What Can Worship Do for Children?

Can it meet real needs in their lives? In this throw-away world described so vividly in Alvin Toffler's *Future Shock,* our children need some absolutes to which they can cling when their environments shake and splinter around them. What is God's answer to these changing times?

Absolutes! The Bible is full of absolutes. Read through a few of them to get a warm, secure feeling:

The only God (1 Tim. 1:17)

Who alone possesses immortality (1 Tim. 6:16)
Only begotten Son (John 3:16)
Who alone works wonders (Ps. 72:18)
That they may know Thee, the only true God (John 17:3)
To the only God, our Saviour (Jude 25)
Thou alone art holy (Rev. 15:4)
Who lives forever and ever (Rev. 4:9)
He will reign forever and ever (Rev. 11:15)
The one who does the will of God abides forever (1 John 2:17)
The Word of the Lord abides forever (1 Peter 1:25)
Thy throne, O God, is forever and ever (Heb. 1:8)
Thou [Christ] art a priest forever (Heb. 5:6)
He always lives to make intercession for us (Heb. 7:25)
He has perfected for all time those who are sanctified (Heb. 10:14)
Thus we shall always be with the Lord (1 Thes. 4:17)
If anyone eats of this bread he shall live forever (John 6:51)
The Word of our God stands forever (Isa. 40:8)

An everlasting salvation (Isa. 45:17)
[The Lord is] the everlasting God . . . Creator (Isa. 40:28)
He who hears and believes has eternal life (John 5:24)
[Jesus] has given us eternal comfort (2 Thes. 2:16)
Having an eternal Gospel to preach (Rev. 14:6)

I am the first and I am the last (Isa. 44:6)
I am the Alpha and the Omega, the beginning and the end (Rev. 21:6)

Jesus Christ is the same yesterday and today, yes and forever (Heb. 13:8)
Thou art the same, and Thy years will not come to an end (Ps. 102:27)

For the same Lord is Lord of all, abounding in riches for
   all (Rom. 10:12)
The Spirit searches all things (1 Cor. 2:10)
All things belong to You . . . (1 Cor. 3.21)
He shall wipe away every tear (Rev. 21:4)
Behold, I am making all things new (Rev. 21:5)

Lo, I am with you always (Matt. 28:20)
You . . . always having all sufficiency in everything (2
   Cor. 9:8)
I will never desert you, nor will I ever forsake you (Heb.
   13:5)
He will never allow the righteous to be shaken (Ps.
   55:22)
He who comes to Me shall not hunger (John 6:35)

The one who comes to Me I will certainly not cast out
   (John 6:37)
No one shall snatch them out of My hand (John 10:28)
God is not one to show partiality (Acts 10:34)
I have put before you an open door which no one can
   shut (Rev. 3:8)
They shall hunger no more (Rev. 7:16)
No longer any death . . . any night . . . any curse (Rev.
   21:4; 22:5, 3)
None of those who wait for Thee will be ashamed (Ps.
   25:3)

All nations are as nothing before Him (Isa. 40:17)
Nothing is too difficult for Thee (Jer. 32:17)
Nothing will be impossible with God (Luke 1:37)
Be anxious for nothing (Phil. 4:6)

His understanding is inscrutable (Isa. 40:28)
His greatness is unsearchable (Ps. 145:3)
How unsearchable are His judgments (Rom. 11:33)
The unfathomable riches of Christ (Eph. 3:8)

I am the way, and the truth, and the life (John 14:6)

After considering how we could give this security to our children, we planned a worship service on the theme: God is eternal and unchanging.

As part of that service three groups of Juniors prepared large posters.

Poster 1. Around the outside of the 48″ square cardboard the girls pasted pictures from magazines showing many different aspects of our life that change frequently, such as clothes and cars, cereal, shoe styles, etc. Inside that they placed a circle of pictures of the four seasons, quoting Genesis 8:22, "While the earth remains, seedtime and harvest, and cold and heat, and summer and winter, and day and night, shall not cease." In the center they placed in large letters, "GOD." As they explained their poster, they read the verse, "Jesus Christ is the same yesterday, and today, yes and forever" (Heb. 13:8).

Poster 2: Around the outside of the large cardboard the group pasted pictures from magazines showing the life cycle of man, beginning with a baby and progressing into adulthood. (The leaders found it amusing and the children selected pictures only through young adulthood, with an apparent feeling that life ended there!) They read from James, "What is your life? You are a mist that appears for a little while and then vanishes" (James 4:14, NIV). Inside that circle they made pictures of the four seasons and read Genesis 8:22. In the center were the large letters "GOD" and with this they read one of Paul's great doxology verses, "To the King eternal, immortal, invisible, the only God, be honor and glory forever and ever" (1 Tim. 1:17).

Poster 3: The group fastened a piece of chicken wire over the entire cardboard. To this the fourth grade boys attached all kinds of throw-away items from their homes, such as tooth paste and milk cartons, gum wrappers, etc. They had no trouble covering the whole area. In the center they placed pictures of the four seasons.

In the service the boys removed the throw-away items piece by piece as they named them, and threw them into a waste basket. Then they read, "According to His promise we wait for new heavens and a new earth, in which righteousness dwells" (2 Peter 3:13), at which they removed the pictures of the four seasons, tore each in two and dropped them into the waste basket. They removed the wire, and there in huge beautiful letters on the bare board were the letters "GOD." The boys read, " 'I am the Alpha and the Omega' says the Lord God, 'who is and who was and who is to come, the Almighty' " (Rev. 1:8).

It was an impressive service. The adults had faith to believe that in days ahead the effect of this service would help hold those boys and girls steady in a throw-away world.

Pitfalls to Avoid

A number of pitfalls in teaching and leading children in worship must be recognized and avoided.

Mindless repetition   When asked to analyze the meaning of a familiar hymn, young adults said, "I didn't know what I was singing" / "I never thought about the words before" / "I don't know what it does mean!" If we've been attending services regularly, we've probably all mouthed the clichés, the familiar words vaguely understood.

How amazing that we can go on repeating words without

knowing their meaning! Many of us formed the habit in childhood, when so much of the church vocabulary was above our heads. We took on so easily the form of godliness without the power thereof (See 2 Tim. 3:5). If we say the same table grace at every meal, we can soon be thinking of something else as we recite the words. We can say the Lord's Prayer without praying it. Routine can breed verbalism without thought. The fault was apparent among God's people in both Old and New Testament days. Jesus quoted Isaiah, "This people honors Me with their lips, but their heart is far away from Me" (Matt. 15:8).

Yet God insists that those who worship Him must worship Him in spirit and in truth (John 4:24). Paul said, "I desire to speak five words with my mind, that I may instruct others also, rather than ten thousand words in a tongue" (1 Cor. 14:19), and "I shall pray with the spirit and I shall pray with the mind also; I shall sing with the spirit and I shall sing with the mind also" (14:15). It's so easy to fall into a thoughtless routine! We sit idly, listen passively, without any response within us—and hence do not worship.

Newness   Sometimes newness prevents worship. If we don't know the song, we must concentrate both on the words and the music. Our minds are focused on "what-comes-next," not on directing our song to God. We must know the song well enough to be able to think of the meaning and make it our own expression. Worship materials should be familiar.

Inappropriateness   But what if the song does not express our feelings at all? What if we cannot enter into the writer's mood? Many songs and prayers chosen for children are not within their grasp intellectually or their range emotionally. "A Mighty Fortress Is Our God" is a majestic hymn, full of profound theology, but its content is beyond most children. Selection is a task the leader must face courageously.

Teaching   Perhaps the most common pitfall for the leader of children is the temptation to teach, rather than to lead into worship; to tell, rather than to elicit a response toward God.

How do you avoid pitfalls? Some or all of the following suggestions should be helpful.

- Face the difficulties squarely. Be aware and watchful.
- Conciously determine which parts of the program are instruction, and which worship.
- Keep asking, "What are we doing that is directed toward God?"
- Consider carefully what purpose the "content" part of the worship service achieves. Does it lead to a face-to-face meeting with God?
- Ask, "Are we going beyond talking about God to talking with Him?"
- Teach the song before worship until it is familiar enough to be used as worship.
- Avoid overuse so the meaning is lost.
- Vary introductions to songs.
- Vary methods of prayer.
- Make "vitality" a watchword.

Kinds of Worship

We worship God alone.
We worship God in the group.

But even if we are with a group, worship must be individual, for only the individual can meet God. This is holy ground for a human leader. The record of God's people from the beginning of human history reveals that God has met people alone and in groups, and that His plans included both kinds of worship. Undoubtedly David first experienced and wrote his psalms as his personal response to God. Then they became group expressions. But there are various kinds of worship, experienced both alone and in a group.

Spontaneous worship   Mother came in to pick up one-year-old Cathy after her nap. Cathy smiled and reached up her arms. With the baby in her arms, Mother raised the shade. A bright beam of sunshine fell across them. Cathy waved her arm in it. Mother said softly, "Thank You, God, for the lovely sunshine."

By the time she was five, Cathy quite naturally included praise to God in her expressions of pleasure. The whole family found it natural to sing a praise to God as they rode to church, or enjoyed a picnic. Cathy was *taught* to make worship spontaneous, a part of everyday life. Her life-style will include it.

The more real experiences of worship a child has, and the more resources for worship he knows, the more likely he is to worship spontaneously. How much Scripture does he know, not by rote words alone, but by understanding and entering into its mood? How many spiritual songs are part of his thinking and feeling? How much freedom in prayer has he experienced? These all are resources likely to aid his spontaneous worship.

Private worship   By the age of four or five a more disciplined regular time of worship can be introduced. Cathy had found Mother and Father at various times with Bible in hand, reading, or engaged in prayer. This prepared her for the suggestion that she could spend some time with God by herself each day. Together Mother and Cathy made some pages for a booklet, fastened together with rings and hung at the head of her bed. On one page was a picture of the family, on another a missionary friend she knew, on another the pastor, also a well-known person. Each week they fastened her Sunday School paper into the booklet removing the previous Sunday's paper. Mother and Father helped Cathy think about the Bible story, memorize the memory verse, and pray in accordance with the lesson. Her parents also took care to suggest varying needs of the family so that she would not merely "bless" each one routinely each day. From time to time they asked her to pray about specific needs for them and for herself.

True, Cathy did not have devotions every day, and Mother did not nag. But Mother sometimes found her in the middle of the morning with her booklet in hand, earnestly looking at the pages.

As Cathy learned to read, her parents placed simple Bible story books and children's devotional books on the table by her bed. But again, they exerted no pressure. So from early years, Cathy frequently experienced a quiet time with the Lord. When she received Christ as Saviour, she began consciously to live for Him; beginning each day with Him was an easy pattern to follow. She testified as a young person that she usually thought of God when she woke up. Yet she did not feel bound legalistically to have a quiet time lest her day should not go well.

Services Planned for Worship

What kinds of worship services are there? It's interesting to ask people to recall a time when they truly worshiped. Do you think of a planned formal service in the church? What part of the service? Was the moment a result of planning? Can the Holy Spirit work in a formal service which is planned and printed in the bulletin?

Obviously most Christians believe so. The pastor works hard on his sermon, believing his flock will not be well fed with extemporaneous preaching—if he just opens his mouth and lets the Lord fill it! To say we can't worship through a planned service leaves worship completely spontaneous, spasmodic, and subject to circumstances. To have the Holy Spirit work, must there be a disruption of plans? Can He use a carefully thought through form that leads in thought to a climax of feeling or decision? Are not evangelistic services so planned and used by God?

Should not the Holy Spirit be consulted in the planning? Should not the service be planned in line with the way God made man to learn and feel and react? Clear ideas, clear procedure, clear continuity are God's ways, for He is not the author of confusion.

Are we any more likely to encourage children to worship if there is not careful thought and prayer behind what we do in leading them to meet the Lord? So often it seems that churches, where adults are led step by step to the climax of the service, will have leaders for the children who combine hit-and-miss singing, praying, and various activities, and call these worship. The Holy Spirit will help us plan a service to bring children into God's presence; He does not do it for us. We must use our minds.

Does experience with a formal service lead to the ability to worship spontaneously, informally, or does spontaneous worship lead to ability to appreciate the formal service? Undoubtedly it works both ways. And both kinds of worship need to be experienced.

Most children's services will be of an informal type in which the service is planned, yes, but the children respond, participate, and are involved in the service. They answer questions, and engage in discussion, which are not usually done in the adult service. While the service is therefore more flexible than one for adults, it is planned thoughtfully. If the children are allowed to choose all the songs, and take the lead, their suggestions will not follow a worship theme nor lead to a conclusion that inspires a change in life.

The Johnsons had stopped at a drive-in for hamburgers. As they sat in the car, the sky became vivid with the colors of the descending sun—red, orange, yellow—so bright the family felt bathed in the colors. Six-year-old Donna said in an awed voice, "In the beginning God created the heavens and the earth."

"Let's sing 'I Sing the Mighty Power of God,' " said nine-year-old Tom. The family sang softly. Then Father began "How Great Thou Art" and everyone joined him.

Behind these instances of informal, spontaneous family worship lay years of careful, prayerful planning, teaching, and experiences.

2

Who Can Worship?

Can an unsaved person worship? The answer may be in another question. Does the unsaved person *want* to worship? If he seeks God's face, he is on his way toward a saving relationship, isn't he?

But what about children? What about those who are too young to have come to knowledge of salvation? Scripture springs to mind:

O Lord, our Lord, how majestic is Thy name in all the earth,
    Who hast displayed Thy splendor above the heavens!
From the mouth of infants and nursing babes Thou hast
    established strength (Ps. 8:1-2).
You have taught the little children to praise You perfectly.
May their example shame and silence Your enemies
    (Ps. 8:2, LB).

When the enemies of Jesus heard the children crying out in the temple, "Hosanna to the Son of David!" they said, "Do You hear what these are saying?"

Jesus was aware. He answered, "Yes, have you never read, 'Out of the mouth of infants and nursing babes Thou hast prepared praise for Thyself'?" (Matt. 21:15-16) They were small children, and it was praise to Him.

Can we perhaps agree that theologically a child who has

not rejected Christ, a child who loves God, can worship acceptably on his own level?

Unsaved Children in a Group

What about the unsaved child who is not merely immature spiritually, but is able to understand the Gospel? This child, we may feel, is responsible. Can we ask him to worship? What can we do when such children are in a group whom we are leading in worship?

Surely our first directive is to present the Gospel simply and clearly, in varied ways.* One time we can expand on the idea of sin, another time on the substitutionary atonement of Christ, so that each part of the Gospel is clarified. But we cannot turn our worship services solely into evangelistic services. The children who have received Christ are ready to be led into worship experiences.

Let's bring in the Gospel, then, but keep the emphasis on the needs of the majority of the group. Can we, when we have the children together in small groups for activities, place together in one group the unsaved, and discuss with them what the Gospel means? We certainly can. All the cautions of working with children in this vital area must be observed, since children are easily pressured by adults. They want to please, may not fully understand, and are emotionally moved when they don't understand. They will respond just to move physically or to get attention or to receive any small gift of a Testament or even a tract.

The invitation should be given in a way to seek out only those with whom the Spirit of God is dealing. He must be working if the child is to be saved. In a group, an invitation may be given for those interested to remain after the others leave; or they may be encouraged to make an appointment with the leader to talk about it; or we can arrange the program so that there is a time when a child can go to one leader to talk about salvation, perhaps when the others are engaged

---

* For help in leading children to Christ and giving follow-up, see Mary E. LeBar, *Living in God's Family,* Scripture Press Publications, Inc. (Cat. No. 6-2252), $2.50.

in a handwork project or working on their worship notebooks.

A child should also know that he can receive Christ as his Saviour at any time or place, all by himself. Urge the children, if they do this, to share this decision with a leader so that he may help them know what to do next. This allows for proper checking of the child's understanding, and for follow-up.

And let's never forget the power of prayer, and the need for prayer if we are dealing with spiritual matters.

Spiritually Immature Children in a Group

"But," a leader says, "some children are not interested in worship because they are spiritually immature, not because they aren't ready for salvation. What do I do with such children?"

Probably the answer is that we must make allowances for them. If all the children in the group are like this, we could say, "Put the worship at their level. Have more movement, more activity, shorter services."

But if such children are a minority in a group, it is more difficult to gear the service to their level. However, awareness of each individual will enable leaders to provide for such children in planning. Give them the active roles. Plan a part they can enjoy. Commend them for being quiet when older boys and girls are worshiping, even if they don't feel like it. If the worship is during church, a children's program is certainly easier for them to enter into than an adult church service, and they can learn to exercise self-control.

Children can and should worship. It is our responsibility as leaders to help them do it.

3

How Can We Prepare Children for Worship?

Basic preparation for worship is of course a knowledge of God. This involves long-range growth in understanding, and the catching of adult attitudes. Every lesson from Scripture teaches us something about God: who He is, what He does, His relationship to people. Every lesson application relates God to us personally. And every Christian adult in the child's environment is also teaching about worship—negatively or positively. Does the teacher or parent radiate love for God, joy in prayer, delight in singing songs to God, consciousness of God's presence? Or does the child catch the unconscious transmission of a feeling of boredom? Or is church-going just out of duty or because of what people will think, or mere routine?

The four- and five-year-olds had just heard the story of how God took care of Elijah. "Aren't we glad God is so kind?" the teacher asked. "Would you like to tell Him so?" Thus prepared, most of those young children had a moment of worship.

Older boys and girls can learn how to prepare their own hearts for a worship service—in attitude, as well as knowledge. What does it mean to worship "in spirit and in truth"?

The primaries learned that when the quiet music began, it was a signal for them to stop talking, and come to the worship corner. There they were invited to hum the worship song being played, and then have a few seconds of complete silence when everyone was asked to pray, "Help me, Lord, to think about You."

To vary this, the leader sometimes would hold up a picture of Jesus with boys and girls, and invite the children to pretend they were one of those children, a particular one, who had come to see Jesus. After a pause, she'd say softly, "We can't see Him, but He promises to be here now. Let's sing to Him, and talk to Him, and love Him right now."

The leader of the juniors in Junior Church put on two glove puppets, and bent her hands over the top of a flannel board.

PUPPET 1: I don't want to worship.

PUPPET 2: I think I know why!

PUPPET 1: You do? Why?

The leader stopped, and asked the group, "What do you think he answered?"

She gave the juniors a few minutes to write down what they thought PUPPET 2 said. (Writing served to help them formulate their answers clearly.) Invited to complete the puppet skit with her, numbers of the juniors were eager to do so. They filled in such answers as:

Because you'd rather watch the TV.

Because you'd rather play ball outside.

Because you'd rather ride your bike.

Most of the answers involved some physical activity rather than being quiet in church. After an hour in Sunday School, these juniors were quite honest; it was hard—it *is* hard—for children to spend the whole morning with so little movement. Leaders were alerted to the fact that they should provide as much freedom of movement and change of pace as possible when expecting children to remain in church for two to three hours.

The leader commented that there was another reason no one had mentioned. She asked them to complete a sentence beginning with: "I worship when I . . . " The answers included:

talk to God.

tell God I love Him.

praise God.

After compiling a list of worship activities on the flip chart, the leader asked, "Who can do this? Who would want to do this? Who would not want to do it?"

It was easy for the children to see that non-Christians would not want to worship, that only those who loved God and were saved would be interested at all.

"But even Christians need to get ready for worship," the leader continued. "And sometimes we don't feel like it. Can you think of another reason we haven't mentioned? (No one could.) Let's turn to Psalm 139 to find it. Read verses 23 and 24 to yourselves and discover a reason."

On the flip chart the question she printed under the reference was: "Is everything right between God and me?":

"Perhaps you have searched your heart," said the leader, "and you do find something there . . . perhaps disobedience to parents, or anger or unkind words at home, what can you do?" This was more familiar ground to the group. The next sheet of the flip chart had 1 John 1:9 printed on it with the words, "Ask forgiveness."

"But if everything is right between you and God, you may still feel you'd rather be playing ball or watching TV. That's not strange. We don't always feel like going to bed when it's time, do we? Or doing the dishes? Or maybe getting up in the morning on time? But we do it. We do it by an act of our will. Perhaps we should say Psalm 9:1 with the psalmist." The children read it together from their Bibles, and on the third sheet of the flip chart the leader wrote the reference and these words: "Decide to worship (I *will*)."

She continued, "Have you ever come to a worship service not feeling much like praising God, but then as you began to sing you began to enjoy it? If we think about what we're singing and saying, we will probably be able to worship the Lord with our whole heart before we get through." She added these words to sheet 3: "Think about God."

"You have learned many things about God. If you begin to think about them, you won't find it hard to worship Him. Try it!"

And the leader inwardly reminded herself that reality in worship for these children was partially her responsibility, together with other adult leaders. They must provide a service at the children's level, of interest to them in their stage of development, related to their lives.

As preparation for the next worship service, the children were asked to consider silently each of the steps. A year later when they were asked how to get ready to worship, the children's responses showed that their understanding was clear and real. After that, a reminder and a quiet pause enabled them to prepare themselves.

4

Family Worship

Support from Scripture

Nowhere does the Bible say, "Thou shalt have family worship each day for half an hour beginning at 6:30 P.M." But in order to fulfill scriptural goals many parents recognize that they need to have family worship. Moses suggests a vital form of spiritual fellowship, admonishing parents to teach their children diligently, to talk of God's revelation at all times of the day, and to have visual reminders in the home and on the person (Deut. 6:5-7). This is better than a set time each day—if by having a set time Christian conversation becomes relegated only to family worshiptime, and does not permeate the lives of the family.

While the most powerful teaching is by life, words must also be used, and more is needed than those which can accompany physical activities. Times of quiet attentiveness are necessary especially if the family is to go beyond instructions to response in worship.

Jesus gave a lovely promise especially fitting to the family unit. "Where two or three have gathered together in My name, there am I in their midst" (Matt. 18:20). Malachi tells us that God desires godly offspring (Mal. 2:15). How do we produce them? Surely there must be spiritual fellow-

33

ship. Paul clearly instructs fathers to bring their children up in the discipline and instruction of the Lord (Eph. 6:4). Other general directives for the Christian life would require the discipling of children in the home for their fulfillment, such as hiding God's Word in the heart to avoid sin (Ps. 119:11) and the instruction to Timothy to study the Word (2 Tim. 2:15). One or two hours in a week in church cannot mold the life sufficiently to accomplish such biblical goals.

What to Accomplish in Family Worship

In a day when the family is flying apart with different schedules even in early school years, a strong spiritual tie is worth much effort. The following testimonies from college students illustrate some of the values of having regular family worship:

"I never had any doubt about what my parents believed. Family worship, and the way they lived, told me. I've never been able to get away from it."

"When I complained about family worship because it kept me from the ball game outside, my parents explained that spiritual food was more necessary than physical food, and it was their responsibility as parents to see that we had both kinds. We didn't doubt the importance of spiritual things."

"Brother-sister quarrels just had to get solved when we had family worship. It was pretty awful when neither my brother nor I would pray. We learned a lot about applying Christian love and forgiveness in some of those sessions."

"We had family prayers before we went to school in the morning, and it really started the day off with a consciousness of God's presence with me."

"God was important in our home. So it didn't seem out of place to honor Him with a special time of praise and prayer each day. Of course sometimes we didn't have our worship-time, but usually we did. I want the same kind of atmosphere for my children."

"Our family found worshiptime valuable, because we always took up things that were of concern to us right then, like a broken toy or a sick friend or a problem in school."

"I especially remember the songs in our family gatherings. We all like to sing, and we learned hymns and made up songs, and generally had a great time praising God. It made a difference in my attitude toward going to church, I'm sure."

"When I went away to school, I faced some real temptations I hadn't known at home. The memory of our praying together, and knowing they were still praying for me regularly, was a real strength to me."

While we acknowledge that the family must instruct in the Word, can't we leave worship for the church? No, we can't! Here's why:

1. Many children's groups do not achieve real worship; like other church agencies, they too are merely instructing.

2. Leading a group of children into God's presence, so that each individual truly knows His presence and communicates with Him, is much harder to do in a large group than in the home setting where there are fewer people involved.

3. The church group cannot focus on the real needs of each individual as well as the home. It's harder for all to participate in a large group.

4. The problem of Tuesday is not in the child's mind by Sunday, but in the family Tuesday's problem can be prayed about on Tuesday.

5. Those who know us best should be the ones who can lead us into real worship.

6. To worship at home makes God a part of everyday life, not a special topic for a special day.

Almost every reason for worshiping at church has greater advantages if done at home. True, worship with a peer group can have its joys. Materials can all be at the right level. And there's support in knowing that others, not only one's family, reverence and adore our God. But at home, worship can grow out of life itself so that a child is comfortable talking about God in any situation.

Beginning Family Worship

The ideal time to start is before any children arrive. Goals and plans should be formulated during this period. With the advent of the first baby, Mother and Father can stand by the crib daily, pray for the baby by name, perhaps repeat a Scripture promise together, such as Proverbs 22:6, and pray for themselves. Who can say how soon the infant comes to sense the presence of God in that quiet moment?

If parents decide to begin when the children are already of school age, a good family discussion should precede the first time of worship. This conference should show the children why their family wants to follow such a practice. It will allow them to share in decisions about the time and place for it, and to make suggestions as to what they would like to do in the worshiptime to honor God.

Does the family know another Christian family who already have a worshiptime that the children enjoy? Perhaps they would be willing to come to the home, lead both families in worship one evening, and discuss what they do for variety and vitality. The church may take the lead in initiating such visits, especially for families where parents are new Christians and feel unsure of themselves in the area of spiritual leadership for their children.

Ages 1-3   The toddler will soon be able to carry the Bible carefully in both hands to Father. He can snuggle in Mother's lap, and, though he doesn't understand anything except the peaceful atmosphere, he feels deeply the togetherness of spirit. He can bring a songbook, or sit by Mother on the piano bench. He can sing his own brand of words, joining in with "a joyful noise unto the Lord." Soon he can thank God for one specific thing each day.

And then perhaps he can depart the worship scene to play quietly with his toys within sight of a parent. Sometimes he may choose to sit quietly with his parents as they continue on an adult or older child's level. But he should not be forced to sit through the whole time. His attitude toward worship at this early age is what is important. When His growing body craves movement (according to God's plan of development), he does not learn to worship by being made to sit still.

When he begins to attend the Nursery class at church, the family can sing a song he is learning there, and talk about his memory words, during the first part of their worshiptime.

"I am so grateful to the church for sending home the Nursery songs," said one mother. "Phil loves to get his book and have us all sing one of his songs. It makes him feel he is important in the family circle."

Usually the child's songs appear in his Sunday School paper or workbook, or may be secured in a Nursery song-book. Probably his paper from church also shows a picture that he can share with his family.

With ages 4 and 5 These children can participate even more. They might show a Bible picture of the Scripture being used, or display a picture they have drawn earlier at Mother's suggestion to illustrate the application of the Scripture being studied by the family. One of their songs and memory verses may be used, probably the one they had last week in Sunday School. This may well be repeated each day for a week, varying the discussion about its teaching and application. Such verses as "Let us love one another," are equally good for every member of the family. Each one could tell when he needs help from God to obey that verse, and then family members could pray for each other.

Sometimes Mother can guide the child to model in clay something to relate to the Bible study of the day. Or he may bring in some object from nature for which to praise the Lord. With a parent's help in remembering, he can tell of a good time God gave him that day, or voice a petition. He can begin to pray for others' needs which he can understand.

"Please, God," Monty prayed, "help Jane pass the test. It's very important."

Devotional materials for this age have many pictures and short Bible stories, or stories to apply Bible truth.

With school-age children Children who read can begin sharing in leadership by reading from simple devotional materials; they can use their Sunday School materials, and soon read from a large-print Bible or a modern language Bible or a paraphrase. Mark is a good Bible book with which to begin. Matthew and Luke have difficult genealogical tables at the beginning, and John has difficult abstract concepts, but Mark quickly gets into action and contains more narrative. Children's devotional materials will also point out selected portions of Scripture which are within a child's grasp. Why not visit Christian bookstores from time to time to obtain quality devotional books for children!

With mixed ages in the family   When a family has for example, a two-year-old, a seven-year-old, and a ten-year-old, the problem of making worship real and stimulating to each member requires thought, ingenuity, and planning.

The following is the testimony of one who came out of an ideal childhood situation:

"In our family the oldest was sometimes invited to read a modern paraphrase after Father read the passage, or he was the one to explain what it meant. Eight-year-old Debbie sat by five-year-old Susan and showed her where we were reading.

"Sometimes each member of our family took one day during the week to be in charge, even the youngest ones under Mother's guidance. Each one could present anything he wanted to, or thought the family needed. Things got rather personal at times, but I suppose that's exactly what worship should be! We had some real discussion, which our parents directed toward prayer, and we ended feeling a problem was solved. Usually, however, each one would tell the others about his Sunday School or church group subject, and we'd pray and sing about that subject. Under our parents' leadership, we learned to turn these subjects into occasions for praising God, so we didn't just teach our lessons, but worshiped God for whatever the lessons revealed about Him.

"We went over the memory verses, and each one in the family tried to say how the verse could apply to his life. Some of the pre-primary verses, like 'Let us love one another,' put all of us on the spot, as we thought about people we found hard to love. We learned not to look down on the simple truths Johnny had in his lessons!"

With varying ages, Father must try to involve each one in some way. Everyone can enjoy playing a Bible story now and then; truth can become more real even to adults. Children's songs convey truths that can speak to all ages, if parents engender the right attitude toward them. After singing "Jesus Loves Me," for instance, each one could tell when he especially needed to remember Jesus' love during his day. Older children will enjoy teaching songs they know and leading the family in activities they've enjoyed at church. In the process the truth becomes more deeply impressed on them.

When parents keep in mind the goals in family worship of reality, vitality, and variety, they will find their children eagerly participating in family worship.

Time

It's always true that we have time for what we consider most important. Few of us miss many meals for lack of time. For worship with children, the hour most families find best is early evening, following dinnertime. Some, however, are able to gather the family in the morning before school.

If a church will encourage all its families to have a family worship at the same approximate time, and discourage people from phoning each other during that time, a start can be made. If Father commutes to work and must leave early and get home late, the problem becomes greater.

Families where Father's presence during the week is impossible may choose to have a lengthier time for family fun and worship on Saturday or Sunday. Mother may hold a regular time with the children before they go to school, or with small ones at any convenient time during the day.

Outsiders and Interruptions

Johnny's second grade friend Rusty arrived early to go to school with him one day. So Mother asked Rusty if he'd like to join them in worship. He sat quietly but made no comment. The next day Rusty arrived early again, and the next. Mother realized that he was coming purposely to join in their prayertime. She welcomed him, and increased the spiritual instruction to meet his needs also. And, of course, the day came when Rusty chose Jesus to be His Saviour and Lord.

Guests in the home give occasion for wider fellowship or witness. Family worship should not be given up when outsiders are present, but should include them in its benefits. Few indeed are the people who object to being prayed for.

Then there's the phone. And the doorbell. If possible, don't meet in a room where there is a phone. One person may be delegated to slip out to answer it, taking any message and offering to call back. At the door the situation can be explained, the person invited to join the worship or wait in another room. We can take such interruptions as opportunities to witness rather than as embarrassments.

Location for Family Worship
Usually families choose a living room setting for comfort and a relaxed atmosphere. But one element in getting reality through variety may be to utilize many locations. In the backyard on a fine evening, at a picnic spot, in a boat on the lake, in different rooms in the house, on the back porch, in the car, in a nearby park, each setting can add something to the experience by suggesting different aspects of God's nature and work. The birthday person might choose where to have family worship. Or the child who is leading may select where in the house the family will meet (within reason).

What to Avoid in Family Worship
Parents frequently find it tempting to discipline by reviewing the child's misbehavior or reprimanding him in prayer. Any value is more than offset by the likely danger that the child will resent this reporting of his conduct to God, and will dislike the idea of prayer. If a parent is to do such reporting in prayer, he should also more often tell God of the child's good behavior, of instances of obedience. But who ever heard a parent do that!

Similarly, preaching by way of prayer can only make prayer

unpleasant. And long prayers are boring. Better many short prayers with everyone participating than one long prayer.

Away with dullness when we're approaching the Creator of life and light and beauty! Away with monotony and dragging when we're with the One whose Book reveals so much activity, and who made children with growing bodies to crave movement! Away with excess formality when He wants to be part of real life and its problems, its tears, and its laughter!

5

Children in the Adult Church Service

There are probably two major reasons why children are in the adult service rather than in children's services.

One is the lack of personnel to carry on children's worship. It is a sacrifice for most adults to leave the morning service, to say nothing of all the work and preparation that must go into a good children's service week after week.

The second reason is that many adults think children should be in the family pew, learning to sit still. This reasoning is as fallacious as thinking that practice will help a two-month-old baby to walk. We cannot push development physically, spiritually, or mentally beyond the limits God has set for the developing person. Even if we insist on a small child sitting still in the seat for the very long adult service, we cannot control his inner being. What is happening there?

Too many memories of adults are only negative with regard to church attendance in their childhood. They remember being bored, counting lights and other parts of the church interior, hating the arrival of Sunday morning, and worst of all, of learning to tune out what was being said. Said a young father, "I'm still having a problem about the ease with which I can sit through a sermon, unconsciously turning it off. I believe it is because I learned to do that in my childhood."

An hour is a very long time for a child. How many parents would like to sit with dangling legs for a comparable period of time, which would be at least twice as long? The child probably also has no back rest, as the seat is too wide for him. Restaurants are more thoughtful of children!

If a child has been forced to sit through meaningless services while he is small, by the time he is able to grasp something of the service, he is all too likely to have formed the habit of not listening. The vocabulary is not his, the concepts are too hard, and immobility is contrary to the crying needs of his physical body.

But what is the parent to do if there is no suitable service at a child's level? Let's consider the situation.

Some parents see that their small child has lively physical action before church, so sitting will be a restful change. Some parents feel it helps attention to sit up front where the pastor and choir and organ are near. Parents can see that the small child is comfortable, physically, and that he has something to do, at least during the sermon. He can color and draw quietly, with effort not to disturb other people who want to think about what the pastor is saying. He can be encouraged to listen for the words of the songs sung, the choir number, and what the pastor talks about. He should be given approval for anything he gleans from the service. If older family members discuss the sermon on the way home, he will want to be a part of the discussion. Perhaps he can only ask a question about something he did hear, but this should be commended, as it shows he tried to listen.

If ahead of time the parents will find out what Scripture the pastor will use for his sermon, the family can read it at home, and try to think what the pastor may say about it. What does the pastor think they all need to learn from it? Then on Sunday, listening will become very active in the family pew, with everyone turning to smile at Father as the pastor voices just what Father thought he might say. As soon as a child can write, he can be encouraged to take notes, so that at home he can contribute something he heard.

Some churches foster a Stay-for-Church Club for children six to eleven. They provide worksheets at two levels of difficulty, so children may pick up one in the lobby as they enter church. Older children fill in the questions on the sheet, which may ask how many times all the people prayed, what one song title was, what the choir sang about, one story or idea from the sermon, and so forth. Younger children may draw a picture related to the theme of the service.

Club members deposit these sheets in the lobby after church. At the end of a period of 10 weeks or so, those who have filled out a required number of sheets are invited to a special Saturday lunch with the pastor and the other Stay-for-Church Club members. Games or crafts and food with the pastor and other church staff can make these spiritual leaders personal friends, whose words are then of far more interest to the children because they know them as people.

A side benefit is that the pastor becomes more aware of the children and what they are gleaning from the service. He may become sensitized to include them in his applications, rather than seeming oblivious of their presence as so many pastors apparently are. If a church does not provide this service—most have never heard of it—parents can provide their own sheets for filling in, and encourage their child to keep a church notebook at home.

If parents are noncritical about the sermon and the church, and if they discuss what in the service helped them to worship the Lord, the children will follow along this path too.

Are there any Christian symbols in the church? A family, may study the meaning of these, or the pictures in the windows, or even the meaning of having the pulpit placed where it is. The symbols will help their child think of these truths as he gazes about the church.

Families may study at home hymns that are commonly sung in the church. Parents may explain as simply as possible the church liturgy, such as the Lord's Prayer or Doxology. Then their children can join in on Sunday morning with some idea of what they are saying and singing. The very attitude engendered in going to and from church is important. Children are aware of and imitate adults. Saturday night is important. Preparation then can change Sunday morning from a hectic melee to a day about which the whole family can truthfully sing "O Day of Joy and Gladness."

6

The Use
of Scripture
in Worship

Ears to hear?

Many a good Christian would, if really honest, admit that the reading of the Scripture in each church meeting is usually dull and boring. Since no one else knows what his mind is doing, he may try dutifully to listen, or he may do so passively, or he may freely or slyly wander about his mental gardens. But Scripture reading is a necessity. Since we believe Scripture to be authoritative, important, inspired, we must include it in our spiritual services. But just suppose that during the reading of the Scripture a telepath transmitted the results of his snooping to a bulletin board in front of the congregation; or perhaps to the interior of the pulpit where the pastor could see what was happening in each mind. The church would soon empty!

Children learn early that "the Bible" is one of the "right" answers. Only occasionally are they uninhibited enough as were a number of children in a junior group to mutter, "Oh, not again!" when the teacher said, "Now let's all look in our Bibles."

If we are indignant at the charge that we who believe the Word are bibliolaters, why do we so often act as if to justify the charge? Words without meaning become no more than a mysterious charm against evil. If a child can repeat such verses as John 3:16 and Romans 6:23, is he thereby on his way to heaven? Or at least insured? We say, "Of course not!" but do we act as if we believe it?

After Ezra read the Word of the Lord to the people, they "bowed low and worshiped the Lord with their faces to the ground." But note that it was read only to those "who could listen with understanding." And it was explained: "They . . . [gave] the sense so that they understood the reading" (Neh. 8:6, 2, 8).

We cannot force inner attentiveness, though we may compel the outer person to sit quietly. With children, let's be sure we prepare them to listen to the Word. We can raise a question, suggest a problem for which God has given an answer, or ask what they think God would say about an idea. One of the important directives is:

Give the hearer something for which to listen,
before you read Scripture.

The teacher of juniors says, "Listen to this important verse: 'If we confess our sins, He is faithful and righteous to forgive us our sins and to cleanse us from all unrighteousness.' This means that God can be right in forgiving us our sins because Jesus paid the penalty. Our part is to confess our sins."

But were the children listening to that verse when it was read? What were they thinking then? To say "Listen!" or "This is important" draws attention once, but it soon loses all force and becomes a routine statement.

Suppose the teacher had begun, "What can we do after we're Christians, after our sins have been forgiven, and then we slip and do something wrong? We're really in trouble then, aren't we? But God has a wonderful promise. Let's read it together from 1 John 1:9."

One primary leader said to another, "Sing to the Lord? What shall I sing about?"

The teacher answered, "The Bible tells you." And he read, "O sing to the Lord a new song, for He has done wonderful things!" (Ps. 98:1)

A third grader (who could read well and had been prepared ahead of time) stood up with his Bible open and said, "The Bible tells you, 'Sing to Him, sing praises to Him, speak of all His wonders' " (Ps. 105:2).

The primaries "heard" those verses.

Unless the children listen *actively,* we might as well keep still for they don't hear. "He that has ears to hear, let him hear." Let's always ask ourselves before we begin, "Do they have ears to hear this?" Expressed colloquially, it is, "Are you pushing and pulling, or are they traveling under their own steam?" The latter makes teaching exciting rather than work. The work comes in thinking how to get "active listening." It requires thought, and thinking is hard. But it's worth all the effort in results.

Hearing the Word can lead to worship (1 Cor. 14:25), and worship can lead to a desire to hear the Word. The Ethiopian eunuch came to Jerusalem to worship, and he went away reading the Scripture (Acts 8:27-28).

Once the truth has been established that God speaks to us personally through His Word, we may preface hearing the Word by saying or paraphrasing the Bible words together: "Speak Lord, for Thy servant is listening" (1 Sam. 3:10). Or the verse may be sung. You might invite the children to make up music for it. Sometimes the Word may be referred to as a personal letter to us from our Friend. Or a group may be asked if they are ready to hear what our great God has to say to them today, and a pause given them to prepare their minds to listen.

For Preschool Children

The following suggestions are but a sampling of the unlimited variety that may be given to the use of Scripture with pre-schoolers. The focus of the worship and the Scripture used will suggest their own means of presentation—with thought centered on the meaning.

Prayer related to stories   Perhaps the children have had a number of Bible stories about God's care. Several children hold the Bible pictures, and each one thanks God for His care for the Bible character in the picture. The teacher may follow each by a brief prayer thanking God for His care for us in a comparable situation.

Directed thought   The teacher may say, "As you look at the pictures I'm going to show you, think inside yourself how much God loves people." To soft music, the teacher holds up familiar pictures such as Jesus with children, Jesus performing miracles, and other Bible pictures.

Feeling with Bible characters   The teacher describes the experience of a Bible character familiar to the children, and role plays how this person feels about God, as, "I am Noah. God told me to build a big boat. I obeyed God and He took care of me and my family when the flood came. I love God." A child may select the picture of Noah from among those displayed. Sometimes a child may be able to put himself into the part of a character and tell how he feels about God. (Primaries also may especially enjoy doing this.)

Matching Bible verses with pictures   The teacher quotes one of the Bible verses the children know and invites them to select the picture of a Bible character who obeyed the verse. For "Let us love one another," the picture might be Abraham giving Lot first choice. Then the children might agree on a prayer they could pray, such as "We're glad we can love each other too. Thank You, God."

Relating Scripture to experience   Each teacher will be watching for times when Scripture can be alive in the experience of children. Then association is made and praise given to God. A child who is taking off his coat tells the teacher that his mother was sick but is now well. Together teacher and child praise God, right there by the coat rack.

In the midst of a lesson on being unselfish, a heavy rainstorm distracts the children. The teacher takes them to the window and they watch the rain. The teacher reads from her Bible, "He waters the earth to make it fertile. The rivers of God will not run dry! . . . He waters the furrows with abundant rain. Showers soften the earth, melting the clods and causing seeds to sprout across the land" (Ps. 65:9-10, LB). (Though some of the words are difficult, even younger children will get the intent of the passage.) They can play being lively raindrops splashing down. They can praise God for the rain and what it will do. And then, with tension relieved, they can return to the thought of the day's lesson.

For School-age Children

Selection of verses   Children should learn to use a concordance as soon as they are able to read well. Juniors can look up verses related to the worship theme and select the most fitting verses to use in the service. Primaries can select from two or three verses printed on a sheet of paper.

Posters   Occasionally a verse which highlights something about God in line with the worship service may be made into a poster. All manner of media may contribute to making interesting, attractive, and different posters. Sometimes children may proceed on their own, using a technique they have learned in school.

Murals   God's work in the life of a Bible character, or a leader from church history, or a contemporary Christian leader, or person with an interesting Christian experience, may be pictured in several scenes on a mural. God's work in these lives leads easily to praise and honor of God.

Scientific facts   Juniors especially are collectors of facts, and appreciate God's wisdom and power shown in the discoveries of science. Utilize a child's rock or bug collection to give glory to God for His creative power, His wisdom, His amazing diversity in creation. Use what the children are learning in school to praise God. Unless they are attending a Christian school, scientific facts are not generally being related to God, and need to be. Primaries can praise God for community helpers.

Scripture in experience   Children are impressed by testimonies of actual experiences with God that show Scripture working out in the lives of people. Before vacations, children may be reminded to look for evidences of God's working, and afterward may tell the group about it—if possible, reading a Scripture that helps express the feeling the child had, such as verses in Psalms 8 or 19. Experiences can range from the great sights in nature to contact with warm Christians, with whom the child worshiped as part of God's family, even though these people were strangers (1 Cor. 1:2).

Children can be helped to see God working in daily life, and to honor Him there. Adults who work with children need to be seen as real people who have dealings with God also. Their testimonies will be "heard" by the children with more intensity than will those of many other adults.

Being Bible characters   Children of all ages can be helped to enter into the feelings of Bible characters in their experiences with God. These may be dramatized in many ways, from telling experiences in first person, to showing the experiences with puppets, or some other medium.

A group of primaries made Bible characters from wooden clothespins by making a simple cloth robe which they colored and tied with a piece of string. A small piece of clay made a base. Each group showed one incident in the life of a Bible character that revealed the love of God, and then the children thought how God had shown love to them and praised Him in individual testimonies.

Scripture as prayer   Children can take a verse which extols God and adapt it into a prayer. This may be printed on a large sheet of paper for all to read and consider what it says, and then to pray together if they mean what it says.

A group of juniors adapted Jude 25 to make it their prayer of adoration:

> To You, the only God,
> our Saviour through Jesus Christ our Lord,
> be glory, majesty, dominion, and authority,
> before all time and now and forever. Amen.

Illustrating Scripture with slides   Slides are easily found that are appropriate for various verses on the theme of worshiping our Creator. Small children and first graders will enjoy holding up pictures that illustrate simple verses about nature.

Choral readings   Choral reading to be most effective needs rehearsal, so that differing speeds and emphases bring out the meaning of the words being read. It takes some time for young readers just to learn to read fluently before they begin working on the emphases. If they themselves determine what emphasis is called for, they will more quickly and easily make the Scripture their own expression. Primaries have a repeated refrain in which all the children join, while older children or teachers read the hard parts. But the whole group can help decide on *how* the words should be read and *who* should read each part.

If the whole group is not participating in the choral reading, those not reading should be told what to listen for as the Scripture is read.

Psalm 24 may be done with two choirs of juniors, one asking questions, the other answering. The boys will enjoy making strong loud affirmations of "The Lord of hosts, He is the King of glory!"

The 23rd Psalm may be done by "light" voices through sections 1-6, or as solos, and by "dark" voices as solos in sections 7-12, with everyone joining in on section 13, slowing down deliberately for the last words. "Dark" voices refer to the heavier, lower voices, and "light" voices to those which are higher and lighter. You can determine which group a child should be in by having each one read a line. Don't divide by boys and girls, since the voices of some young boys may be lighter than those of some of the girls.

THE SHEPHERD PSALM

1. The Lord is my Shepherd,
2. I shall not want.
3. He makes me lie down in green pastures;
4. He leads me beside quiet waters.
5. He restores my soul;
6. He guides me in the paths of righteousness for His name's sake.

7. Even though I walk through the valley of the shadow of death,
8. I fear no evil;
9. For Thou art with me;
10. Thy rod and Thy staff, they comfort me.
11. Thou dost prepare a table before me in the presence of my enemies;
12. Thou hast anointed my head with oil; my cup overflows.
13. Surely goodness and loving-kindness will follow me all the days of my life, and I will dwell in the house of the Lord forever.

Isaiah 40:6-9 can be very effectively done if practice makes "the grass withers" fade off, with voices dropping. And so also "the flower fades." Then verse 9 can be loud and slow with "forever" drawn out as long as possible.

For a group of juniors a combination of verses to extol God as King was arranged, using Psalm 24 especially. Four groups stood in the four corners of the room, and the reading went from one group to another to another, back and forth, and all together.

The first time the children did it, the technique was so new and surprising that the children reported in evaluation time that they did not worship during it. The reading was repeated in another service, and then they reported that they could worship God and praise Him with the readers.

This accords with the directive: *worship materials should be somewhat familiar.* New methods should probably be gone over with the whole group in preparation time to introduce them, and a second time to expect worship. We must have variety and freshness, but if a material or method is too new, people are distracted from thinking about God.

The following is a loose paraphrase of Psalm 24, using portions of other psalms for the choral reading. The needed parts are listed below.

SOLOS:	GROUPS:
Dark 1 or Boy 1	Light 1 Choir 1
Dark 2 or Boy 2	Light 2 Choir 2
Light 1 or Girl 1	Dark 3 Choir 3
Light 2 or Girl 2	Dark 4 Choir 4

Each child underlined with a colored pencil or crayon the

places where he was to read. Groups were called choirs, and individuals called by name.

PRAISE TO OUR KING

BOY 1	The earth is the Lord's, and all it contains!
CHOIR 1	The Lord reigns, let the earth rejoice!
CHOIR 2	Shout joyfully to the Lord, all the earth!
CHOIR 3	For the Lord is a great God, and a great King!
CHOIR 2	Worship the Lord in holy array.
CHOIR 4	Tremble, O earth, before the Lord.
CHOIR 1	Lift up your heads, O gates,
CHOIR 2	And be lifted up, O ancient doors,
CHOIRS 1, 2	That the King of glory may come in!
BOY 2	Who is the King of glory?
CHOIR 3	The Lord!
CHOIR 4	The Lord strong and mighty,
CHOIRS 3, 4	The Lord mighty in battle.
BOY 1	The Lord on high is mighty.
GIRL 1	Great is the Lord, and highly to be praised.
CHOIR 3	Sing praises to God!
CHOIR 1	Sing praises!
CHOIR 4	Sing praises!
CHOIR 2	Sing praises to our King!
GIRL 1	Sing praises!
GIRL 2	Sing praises!
BOY 2	For God is the King of all the earth.
GIRLS 1, 2	Sing praises with a skillful psalm.
BOY 1	Lift up your heads, O gates,
BOY 2	And be lifted up, O ancient doors,
CHOIRS 3, 4	That the King of glory may come in!
GIRL 1	Who is the King of glory?
CHOIR 3	The Lord of hosts, He is the King of glory!
CHOIR 1	The Lord is our Lawgiver.
CHOIR 2	The Lord is our King.
CHOIRS 1, 2	The Lord of lords and the King of kings!
ALL 4 CHOIRS	The Lord is King forever and ever!

Making Scripture personal   A boys' group wrote out Bible verses showing how God's love overcame sin, with a place where they could fill in their own names, as,

"But God shows His love for us in that while _____ was yet a sinner, Christ died for _____" (Rom. 5:8).

"See what love the Father has given ＿＿＿＿＿＿ that we should be called children of God; and so we are" (1 John 3:1).

In the worship service focusing on God's love, all the children were invited to read the verses aloud, filling in their own names. Then everyone prayed together, "Thank You, Lord."

Illustrating God as Revealer Fourth- through sixth-grade groups prepared to lead the others in worship of God as He has revealed Himself in history, nature, the Word, and Christ.

For history, using a felt tip pen, a group made a long time-line on a strip of shelf paper, putting in the major historical events which they knew, either as words or as a sketch. Then they adapted the song "God Is So Good" to sing, "God is so good; He works through time."

For nature, a group made a mobile of the planetary system, and as one child held it up, another read, "Since the creation of the world His invisible attributes, His eternal power and divine nature, have been clearly seen, being understood through what has been made" (Rom. 1:20). They led the group in singing, "God is so good; He made this world."

For the Word, a group played a tape on which they had recorded verses about God speaking through His Word. They led in singing, "God is so good; He gave us His Word."

For the revelation of Christ, a group of boys became Bible characters who knew Christ when He was on earth (Peter, Philip, Thomas, Paul, John the Baptist, and John the apostle). One boy interviewed them to learn of their contacts with Christ and what they thought of Him. The group sang, "God is so good; He sent us His Son."

Illustrating God as Judge and Saviour Children made posters of feelings elicited by Scripture on sin and judgment. Jagged red and black papers were built up into a collage. A poster composed of a large triangle of white and a large triangle of black was displayed to illustrate 2 Corinthians 5:10: "We must all appear before the judgment seat of Christ, that each one may be recompensed for his deeds in the body, according to what he has done, whether good or bad."

On a pair of scales, each girl in one group laid something to represent good or bad works. Then the girls placed a small metal cross on the good side, and it outweighed all the other things. They read Scripture about God's gift of salvation, and its relation to works, and then gave a sincere invitation to talk with teachers about salvation. A story followed that showed the importance of even the small things we do that are wrong. The children were ready for silent prayer at the conclusion.

Reading Scripture in parts   Occasionally a story chosen to help with the worship subject has direct discourse in it. Then the group can take parts, and read it as a play. If this is rehearsed so that it is read with expression, it can make the Scripture alive.

Reading various modern-language Bible versions   A primary child sat with Bible in hand, pretending to read. Then he raised his head and said, "Oh, I don't understand that verse!" Behind him, three children each read the verse from a different version or paraphrase. When they finished, the seated child said, "That helps. I'm glad different people have translated the Bible."

Letters from God   Scriptures can be placed in envelopes with canceled stamps from old letters, and addressed to individuals. Then the letters can be delivered during a worship service, and the child asked to share what God has written to him. Or letters may be addressed to the whole group, and read by individuals at the appropriate moment.

Using an overhead projector   If this equipment is available, Scriptures may be printed on transparencies, and then the key phrases or words underlined or circled as they are read in the worship service. Or words can be enlarged, colored, or pictured, with parts revealed gradually.

7

The Use
of Music
in Worship

It's Scriptural!

Our world was born in song. At creation the morning stars
sang together and all the sons of God shouted for joy! (Job
38:7) All through the Bible we find references to singing and
musical instruments—to be used to worship God. What do
these verses say in terms of children?

"All the earth will worship Thee, and will sing praises to
Thee; They will sing praises to Thy name" (Ps. 66:4).

Deborah and Barak sang a duet, "Hear, O kings; give ear,
O rulers! to the Lord, I will sing, I will sing praise to the
Lord, the God of Israel" (Jud. 5:3).

Hezekiah made music an integral and a vital part of worship:

> When the burnt offering began, the song to the Lord also
> began with the trumpets, accompanied by the instruments
> of David, king of Israel. While the whole assembly wor-
> shiped, the singers also sang, and the trumpets sounded. . . .
> Moreover, King Hezekiah and the officials ordered the
> Levites to sing praises to the Lord with the words of David
> and Asaph the seer. So they sang praises with joy, and
> bowed down and worshiped (2 Chron. 29:27-30).

Paul directs Christians to address one another "with psalms

57

and hymns and spiritual songs, singing with thankfulness in your hearts to God" (Col. 3:16).

He further tells us how to sing: "I shall sing with the spirit and I shall sing with the mind also" (1 Cor. 14:15).

These are but samplings of the references to music in the Word of God.

It's for Children

A time filler? Till everyone arrives? Mechanical activity with no thought or feeling? Not if we follow the Scriptures above.

- Is the child's singing truly worship? Does it help him meet God?
- Is it with the mind? Does he think what he sings?
- Is it with the spirit? Is it an offering to the Lord?
- Is it with the feelings? Is he glad? Is he thankful?

Songs can help children say what they cannot find words to express. If the literary and poetic quality is good, the song can lift his soul to worship, stretch his appreciation, and enlarge his worship.

Selection of Songs

To fulfill the above purposes, we must select the songs we have children sing carefully. Rarely will we let the group choose randomly what they want to sing, because neither the choices nor the order will lead them to a focus of worship. Sometimes they may be asked to choose songs on the subject of the worship service.

There is a wealth of good songs and hymns available for use with children, and some in print which are not worthy, requiring caution and thought.

Probably the greatest hindrance to having children sing songs of spiritual value to them is the fact that teachers do not know the songs the curriculum publisher has printed to go with the unit of study. Instead of learning the songs, it is easier to take a short peppy young people's chorus and teach that. But today many of the curriculum songs are on records or tapes so that teachers who can't play the piano can learn them if they really want to. Some "ditty" songs are acceptable, but surely children should learn some songs which could properly be called children's hymns, in that they have better artistry in words and are richer in thought.

What must our criteria be?

1. Does the subject suit our purpose in worship?

2. Is the vocabulary right for the age level? A few difficult words may be taught, but if these are too hard or too many, the children will not remember our explanations.

3. Is the song literal, not figurative or abstract, no matter how beautiful the symbolic expression?

Imagine teaching the following to children:

> His yoke is easy, His burden is light,
> I've found it so, I've found it so;
> He leadeth me by day and by night
> Where living waters flow.

These words do not reflect the experiences nor the feelings of most children. *Yoke* and *burden* are difficult words. But the greatest problem is that *yoke* and *burden* and *living waters* are all symbolic expressions which children usually do not grasp because God has made them to think literally and concretely. *Yoke* and *burden* and *water* are concrete sensory things, yes, but they represent something abstract. Trying to explain them simply will reveal how hard they are. And even after explanation, children will usually not understand because they do not think that way.

And though many Christians have worshiped with the following song, literal-minded children will have problems with:

> There is a fountain filled with blood
> Drawn from Immanuel's veins,
> And sinners plunged beneath that flood
> Lose all their guilty stains.

Many songs in books for children also contain symbolic expressions far better left for later years. Not only do children not grasp the meaning, they form the bad habit of singing without expecting to understand or mean what they say.

4. Is the length suitable for the age level? Songs for two-

and three-year-olds are usually one or two musical scores; four- and five-year-olds manage songs with two to four musical scores; older children can sing songs of adult length, though six- to eight-year-olds probably will learn only one stanza if the song is long.

5. Is the mood one the children can appreciate? Does it express their emotions? Can they feel it?

Consider what realistic, nonsentimental, wise-cracking junior would do with the beautiful hymn adults sing:

> Alas and did my Saviour bleed?
> And did my Sovereign die?
> Would He devote that sacred head
> For such a worm as I?

6. Are the ideas within their grasp?

> Light of the world, we haîl Thee,
> Flushing the eastern skies;
> Never shall darkness veil Thee
> Again from human eyes;
> Too long, alas, withholden,
> Now spread from shore to shore;
> Thy light so glad and golden
> Shall set on earth no more.

Most children would have trouble with that song, purely from the viewpoint of concepts, though most of the words they know or could quickly understand.

7. Let's ask when selecting a song: Will this go into the week with a child, to carry on a spiritual thought, to be a means of praise for him? Can it become his own expression?

"Yes," said an older woman regretfully, "I was in church all my childhood. And I could sing right through the hymn-book without thinking of anything I was singing. It was astonishing to me as an adult to discover the beautiful thoughts, the rich doctrines, the spiritual food that I'd needed and missed all those years. It was in the hymns. I early learned to tune out the words because I was not taught to think as I sang or mean what I was saying."

In a home, Sunday School songs can be used, with each person teaching the others a song he has learned. Older members of the family can ask questions about the words, making sure the youngsters understand what the song means.

Teaching a Song

A new song may be part of worship or not, depending on how it is used. Usually the song is taught before it becomes worship. But the following ideas suggest how a song may constitute both worship and a learning process.

1. The song is introduced as an expression of praise, and the children are given something to listen for, such as, "The man who wrote this song had been outdoors using his eyes and ears. As you listen, which of the things he mentions can you also praise the Lord for?" Then the song may be sung, or played on a tape or record.

2. "Let me call you to worship with a song." The leader then sings a call to worship. After a number of weeks, when the children have absorbed it, they will begin to join in. Then the leader can say, "Let's call each other to worship with our song."

3. "Would you like to praise the Lord silently as I show you some pictures of what He has done?" The leader shows the pictures and sings a song that accompanies them.

The first step in teaching a new song is to introduce it in a setting so that the message is heard. Not, "We're going to learn a new song," but in the preceding illustrated ways, so that emphasis is on the thought. Used so, a song may be part of our worship.

Children need to hear a song a number of times before they are asked to sing it, unless it's merely one or two phrases repeated. And all songs will not want to be of this simplicity. If the children sing it wrong, it's harder to learn it right. Repeated listening may be more difficult to make true worship. But even repeated hearing should be active listening, not passive. The message of the song should be kept uppermost.

For nursery children, the repetition is done conversationally, as a natural part of the leader's talking. The song is "caught" rather than "taught." And its meaning in this process is clear because it has been used meaningfully each time it has been repeated.

As long as repetition is introduced with a reason for listening, a song can be a part of worship. "As you listen this time, thank God for one thing the song praises Him for." Later, "Now this time as you listen, pick another thing to thank God for."

Primary children will appreciate having the words written large on a poster. Juniors may be able to use junior hymnbooks, or their own hymnbooks. The process of illustrating the words of a song, which has been meaningfully introduced, will serve further to teach it. Sometimes children can make drawings to fasten around the words to illustrate them, or a border, or a mural. The drawings may express the feelings of the song rather than its words. Or they may show the outworkings of a song in life.

Before children can read, songs should be taught as wholes, with the words and music together each time, and the whole song repeated each time. This ensures the hearing of the message, not unintelligible bits.

Juniors deserve to learn to know the great writers, like Bach and Wesley and Watts. There are many hymn stories about both the writers and God's use of the songs. Sometimes a work of great art may be studied and related to a hymn.

"Early birds" on Sunday morning may learn a new song and then become a choir to sing it to the others in the worship service as a special number. Some juniors can play an instrument well enough to become special soloists for the worship service.

Children will need some introduction to listening to music without words so that they worship as they listen. Make definite suggestions for their thinking, or they easily become restless.

Sometimes motions may serve to keep listening active while the song is sung several times. But let's make sure these motions emphasize the message of the song, and are not merely activity. (Another danger of symbolic songs is that motions for them are easy but they emphasize the concrete elements, not the message. Thus throwing out a fishline for "I will make you fishers of men" leads the child away from the meaning of the song.)

Each song has its own unique possibility for becoming meaningful, based, of course, on its message. Thus using songs in worship can always be fresh and varied.

Using Known Songs

When the children know a song, they can easily forget what they're singing about, and it can become activity rather than worship. We can't sing a song meaningfully one Sunday, then forever after assume all in the group understand and are thinking about the message. The song should continually be integrated into the unit being taught. Each time a song is sung, it should be a part of the discussion, serve some purpose, have an introduction, no matter how brief, to direct the children's thought.

Compare: "Let's sing page 99" with "Let's tell God how we feel as we sing the song on page 99" / "Can we all pray as we sing 'How Great Thou Art'?"/"Let's call each other to worship as we sing 'O Worship the King' " / "Let's rejoice together as we sing 'What a Friend We Have in Jesus.' "

And if words are difficult, children need re-teaching after a period of time. We need to check occasionally to see what the children think they are saying in the song. How amazing it is to learn that many children didn't even know what they were saying when they sang "Jesus loves me, this I know," but were saying, "Jesus loves me, this sino," and only discovered what the words were after they learned to read. And how many little children sing "For the Bible tells me so," but are quite unable to tell a questioner how they know Jesus loves them —right after they've sung the song! What value is singing if it is done mechanically without meaning? Pleasant activity and togetherness, maybe. Is that enough? It isn't worship.

Children form habit patterns in relation to songs. Will they give attention to the message and enter into it, or be able to think of other things as they sing? If songs are continually introduced by reference to *how* to sing them rather than the message, quite likely the message will not be the focus of thought. Compare "Now let's sing the first part loud, and the last two lines softly" with "We can call each other to worship in the first two lines. Then we're talking to God so let's sing that part to Him as a soft prayer of thanks."

Church Hymns?

The Christian church has a treasure in its hymns, rich in theology and depth of meaning and experience. Surely we want our children to enjoy these as soon as they can. But appreciation comes through understanding and use. Perhaps the primary children can learn a few selected, concrete stanzas, such as a stanza, "Fairest Lord Jesus" and "May Jesus Christ Be Praised." Juniors can study hymns that are vigorous and challenging such as those listed on p. 65. If a hymn is really understood and well known, it becomes a worship vehicle.

Some of the great hymns should be memorized so that they become a repository for meditation. Music aids the memory. And children learn to love what they really know. What of the depth of the songs your children are learning? Will they provide rich food for the soul?

The family can plan to memorize carefully selected hymns, using them in family worship, singing appropriate ones at the table for grace, and singing and discussing a hymn as they journey in the car. One mother called her family to the table by beginning to sing the hymn they were currently learning, and the family members took up the song as they came from various parts of the house.

A concerned teacher reminisces: "My friend grew up in a Christian home where they made a practice of memorizing hymns. She could sing them, quote them, and use them to express spiritual thoughts beautifully. My home was a Christian one, but I felt impoverished in this area, and so envious of her. Of course it's never too late to learn, but I wish I'd had these songs in my mind in my teen years." Songs do stay with a person.

Sometimes hymns *about* God can be made into hymns *to* Him. The words can be revised by the group or the family together, and the revision printed out for the children who can read. So "May the grace of Christ our Saviour" may be sung, "May your love, O Christ my Saviour," addressing Him directly and using a simpler word for children to grasp. Sometimes you may wish to add a new stanza with simpler words and thoughts at the level of the children. Knowing the music and context, the transfer to the adult words will be easy.

Here are a few suggestions of songs for juniors, to illustrate the points made:

Great hymns which require careful teaching of vocabulary and concepts:

A Mighty Fortress Is Our God
The King of Love My Shepherd Is
God of Our Fathers, Whose Almighty Hand
If Thou But Suffer God to Guide Thee
How Great Thou Art
For the Beauty of the Earth
How Firm a Foundation
This Is My Father's World
I Sing the Mighty Power of God
All Creatures of Our God and King

Worship songs of praise worth learning:

Fairest Lord Jesus
Hallelujah, What a Saviour
Jesus the Very Thought of Thee
The God of Abraham Praise
Joyful, Joyful We Adore Thee (Beethoven and Van Dyke)
My God, I Love Thee (Handel and Xavier)
Praise Ye the Lord the Almighty, the King of Creation
Praise Him, Praise Him

Songs of comfort that children can appreciate, if taught:

God Will Take Care of You
Great Is Thy Faithfulness
From Every Stormy Wind that Blows
Guide Me, O Thou Great Jehovah
What A Friend We Have in Jesus

Songs of challenge:

Trust and Obey
Who Is on the Lord's Side?
Lord, Speak to Me
Holy Bible, Book Divine

Happy songs:

Blessed Assurance
I Will Sing of My Redeemer
There's Within My Heart a Melody (1st Stanza)

Illustrations of adapting songs: The second stanza of "Holy Bible, Book Divine" can be changed from "Mine to chide me when I rove" to "Mine to check me when I sin."

"Let Us with a Gladsome Voice" will be simpler if "aye endure" is changed to "will endure."

Modern Songs

The children will enjoy and profit from some of the modern songs being sung to guitars, but these need to be as carefully selected as do the older hymns. It is more difficult to make suggestions about specific songs, since the current repertoire changes so rapidly. Primaries and juniors can enjoy:

"God Is So Wonderful." (It may be made direct praise by singing, "God, You're so wonderful.")

"Happiness Is . . ." and the children may add stanzas.

"God Is So Good."

Using Instruments in Worship

Small children enjoy toy instruments. The family, as well as teachers, can improvise their own band with household noise-makers or easily constructed instruments, such as tambourines made from pie pans with bottle tops attached, or moracas made by putting beans in a can or box, or a scale made by adding water to glasses to tune them.

Older children who take lessons can early dedicate their talents to the Lord, and work hard to learn to play well enough to offer beautiful music to the Lord in praise. At the church, leaders may well set a standard of performance before a child is allowed to play in the worship service for the prelude, or offertory, because children hear good music today and are not helped to worship by crude beginning efforts. Accept the child's playing as a gift to the Lord, and give some guidance to the thought of the group as they listen. Can they follow the words, if it's a song they know, or be given the ideas of the music so they can think about them and praise God?

Music without words should be purposefully and thoughtfully used. What are the children to do while it is being played? They may be helped to discern the feelings which different kinds of music can produce. "This is a happy piece of music. As you listen see if you feel like praising God that He gives so much happiness to us."

Using Tapes and Records

An increasing wealth of materials in the audio area is ready for our use in worship. Leaders who are not musical themselves can use tape recorders to get those who are talented to sing for the children or play their songs. With careful preparation, some parts of great musical compositions, such as the *Messiah,* can be understood and appreciated by children. Perhaps the church choir is presenting a number which the children who are in Primary or Junior Church will not hear, but which they could appreciate—especially if the words were printed out and displayed before them as they listen. Such a number could be tape recorded at choir rehearsal.

Children's records are numerous, but must be evaluated according to the criteria already given for songs. Many of the recorded songs are extremely symbolic and unchildlike in thought, even though they may be short, happy, repetitious, and "fun to sing." The children may enjoy singing with an orchestra when they know the hymn being played. It gives them a sense of producing something beautiful and wonderful.

Creative Music

We do not create like God, out of nothing. So there must be input before we can ask for new arrangements of ideas or experience. Most children have had much exposure to music. Probably the easiest creative work is to ask small children to sing the Bible words with which they have become familiar: "Let us sing to the Lord," or "Be kind to one another," or "Let us love one another." Teachers may set an example by singing directions, as "Now it's time to sit down." Or, "Nancy, can you hang up your coat?" Singing conversationally takes music out of the formal area.

Many children sing spontaneously at their play. It is not

too difficult a step to sing specific Bible words. Once a child has done so, and the teacher has approved him, others will be encouraged to try also. No effort can be labeled "wrong" if it is creative; all should be encouraged. When a felicitous tune is produced, it can be jotted down on music paper, and the whole group learn to sing "Debby's song."

Older children may begin with Scripture too, but be encouraged to write a poem to be set to music. Many children have had experiences in school in writing poetry, if not music,

THE LORD IS OUR KING

HEIDI OLEARI WITH MARY WEBER

HEIDI OLEARI

1. O worship the Al-migh-ty King, the ma-jes-tic King a-bove;
2. O-bey the Al-migh-ty King, And serve Him to-day.

Bring Him an of-fer-ing to show Him our love. The Lord is our
For He rules ev-ery-thing in His own way.

King The Lord is our Sav-iour. He's King of kings, He reigns for ev-er.

ⓒ 1975 by Mary E. LeBar. Used by permission.

and need only a little encouragement. After some initial approval of even crude attempts, a child or group can be guided to work over a "poem" to make it more rhythmic, to give more beautiful expression to a thought, to keep one focus of thought. Creative work should be purely voluntary, but growing talents should not be confined to school subjects or experiences.

In guiding group composition, some suggestions are:

1. Arrange the words so the phrases are not too long.

2. Be sure the first phrase is an easy one.

3. Establish a free open atmosphere.

4. Remember that no creative effort can be "wrong." Give much appreciation and approval for efforts.

5. If a musical phrase is not a pleasing one, have several try and let the children choose the one they like best.

6. Have someone at the piano play the tune and harmonize it. This sounds great and stimulates the group. Also have the person write down the notes so they may be retained. Teachers can easily forget, so do this for even a simple song that nursery or beginner children will sing without the piano.

After a first successful experience, the children will not be afraid of making further attempts. Make the first time pleasant.

"The Lord is Our King" was written by a sixth-grade girl, guided by a musical leader. Her junior group loved to sing it.

A group of sixth-grade girls wrote the words "God's Power." The leader expected only one stanza, but they were enthusiastic and came up with four.

CHORUS: In Your hand are power and might
Over all things in Your sight,
We see Your greatness every hour,
We will sing and praise Your power.

1. He showed His power to create
When He made earth and heaven so great;
He made the moon, the stars, the sun,
Praise Him for the things He's done.

2. See the marvelous things He's done.
He has even sent His Son.
His power over Satan He shows
By sending Christ who died and rose.

3. Christ came to save us from our sin,
   And then someday He'll come again;
   Jesus' death was not in vain
   Because He shall forever reign.

4. If He comes in your heart to stay,
   Then He will never go away;
   If you will let Him just forgive,
   What a wondrous life you'll live.

True, the words contain many clichés, but it was the first attempt of these girls to work together creatively.

A group of five-year-olds already had enough background, perhaps from kindergarten, to suggest having the music echo, when they set a Bible verse to music!

I Am with Thee

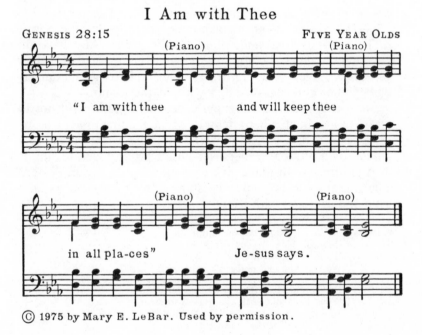

GENESIS 28:15   FIVE YEAR OLDS

A group of primaries wrote the music for Psalm 107:21—and sang it endlessly!

PRAISE THE LORD

PSALM 107: 21   PRIMARY BOYS AND GIRLS

Praise the Lord, Praise the Lord for His good-ness,

Praise the Lord, Praise the Lord for His good-ness,

And for His won-der-ful works to the chil-dren of

men! And for His won-der-ful works to the chil-dren of men!

8

The Use of Prayer in Worship

When to Pray

There is no specific "time" or way to pray. Prayers grow out of experiences and feelings which are raised to a sense of awe, reverence, and praise. Then and then only is prayer heartfelt worship.

If children in a group are not ready to pray, it can be a mockery for the leader to begin to pray anyway, or try to force them to pray. A nursery group was brought by the leader several times to a point of readiness, only to have a child begin to cry, or someone to open the door to disturb the group. It ended by their having no group prayer that hour. This was far better than going through the outward motions when children are not truly praying. (Of course, teachers can pray with individuals whenever they are ready to pray.)

How to Pray

Children should become comfortable with prayer in any and every form. It should be a natural expression of feeling at any time. Therefore worship services will be flexible, even though expected prayer is planned. A leader who is open to the leading of the Holy Spirit will sense a moment when all are ready to turn to God. And he will vary the form, the posture, and the content. Since all levels may use almost all forms and postures, our discussion of prayer will not be divided into age levels.

At any age, the first kind of prayer a child learns should be the spontaneous "talking with God" that does not require any special posture or words, but is a true expression of his feelings. For very young children, this prayer will be short, on one subject. But such prayers may be well used at any level in preference to long prayers covering many areas. Children will not dread prayertime, if prayer is found to be brief and relevant to what is being discussed.

This is true at home also in family worship. Prayers can be conversational much of the time, so that a child does not have to try to pray with Father, if indeed he does try, through a long prayer that includes each child, home needs, relatives and friends, church matters, school problems, and other needs.

Check your use of prayer to see if the children, or family, are making use of:

- individual spontaneous wording
- conversational prayer
- silent prayer
- Scripture addressed to God—or revised to do so
- words of songs addressed to God—or revised to so do
- perhaps words repeated after the leader, for children up to about eight years
- memorized prayers, such as table graces, the Lord's Prayer

  A student, remembering her childhood, said, "Many times I prayed, 'Now I lay me down to sleep . . . if I should die before I wake' and then lay shivering for what seemed hours before I fell asleep, fearful that I'd die in my sleep."

- prayers composed by the group or family

  A group of juniors wrote letters to God around the focus of the morning worship. They read these to the whole group twice, once to see if the group wanted to say the same thing to God, and a second time for those who did, to pray silently the thoughts with them as they read.

  A group of sixth-grade girls held up a long banner on which they'd written many characteristics of God. They had chosen three and written prayers of adoration to God for these. They read these prayers to the group, then had a time of silence for the group to praise God for some characteristic either one the girls had chosen (which set a pattern for the group members who needed it), or for another characteristic on the banner which would be more important to them.

- a litany (where one phrase is repeated by all after specifics, as in Psalm 136) using repeated phrases as "We thank You, God."

    A primary group held, up pictures they had carefully selected and one child said for each picture, "We praise You God, for . . . " with the whole group responding, "We praise You, God!"

Children need help to learn the different kinds of prayer. What is a person supposed to do when someone else is praying aloud? Listen? Then he's not praying. Can he not silently say, "Yes, Lord," when he hears what he wishes to say to God also, or, "Amen," in his heart? Preparation needs to be made for any kind of prayer, discussing what we want to praise God for, or ask Him, not plunging into prayer with "Let's pray," when no reason is apparent.

Often silent prayer is most real because it can be personalized. If worship has been on the subject of salvation, some in the group may need to ask for salvation, and some to thank God for their salvation. They cannot all pray the same thing. Silent prayer may be directed, too, from subject to subject, which helps the child keep praying and to think about what he's praying. "Let's thank God for making each of us well . . . Let's ask Him to heal Tim's mom soon . . . Let's praise Him for our new chairs . . . Let's ask Him to help each of us in what we may find hard today. Tell Him what it is if you think you know."

The most grievous fault of adult leaders is over-emphasizing posture in prayer. Do you introduce prayer with "Now bow your head and close your eyes?" Does posture matter? Is this what we want children to think about when prayer is mentioned?

Posture is to help us. Closing the eyes does help young children concentrate on praying rather than on people around them, especially in a group of children. They can understand and agree on this at an early age. Then it need not be mentioned in each introduction to prayer!

But bowing the head belongs to the idea of submission, perhaps to royalty, and discussion about it is best reserved till a child is old enough to understand and appreciate the explanation. If the adult bows his head, the small child will imitate him anyway. And if he asks, he is ready for an explanation.

"How come," asked a six-year-old, "if God is up in heaven, we have to look down when we pray?"

Must hands be folded? Why? The child can understand that his hands should be where they won't bother other people while we're talking to God, but isn't this enough? Does it need mention every time we pray? Not if the posture is understood and a habit formed.

Let's free he child early to be able to use any posture. Let's kneel. Let's walk with eyes open praying silently to God. Let's sit, stand, hold hands in a circle, or any other posture that seems natural for the situation. Solomon "spread out his hands toward heaven" for his great temple prayer (2 Chron. 6:13). Could we stand on a hillside watching the sunset and do so too? Daniel knelt. The psalmist spoke of being on his bed, and praying in the night.

What to Pray

If we're worshiping, praise for specific good gifts from God is easy. But confession may need to be dealt with first, if we are to be at ease with God. Children can feel this, and should feel it. Praise is hollow if we are guilty in God's presence. Both in the home and in church groups, after clear teaching, a moment of silence may prepare children for worship. (See "Preparation for Worship," chap. 3.) It will be difficult to avoid petition and intercession, but let's make sure we do not let them monopolize our prayers to the exclusion of abundant praise.

Adoration is without question the rarest and most difficult kind of praying. To look at God without immediately thinking of ourselves is hard, as revealed even by our hymnbooks. And this kind of prayer is harder for the younger child, for he is by nature self-centered. Let our aim be to lead the children gradually through praise for concrete things and events until they can praise God for who He is and for specific things He has done for them.

A group of young adults on a day of prayer were asked to spend the first five minutes just looking at God, without reference to themselves. It was impossible for them to do this. Petition crept into almost every prayer that was offered.

But juniors particularly can be helped step by step to have moments of adoration if adults plan carefully to help them. Worship services built around one characteristic of God do help the focus. If each group contributing to the service is motivated by the thought, *How can we help the others to appreciate that God is wise?* (or loving, or kind, or powerful, etc.) they can grow in ability to adore God for who He is.

Leading in Prayer

The leader (teacher or parent) who wishes a group of children to pray with him will try first to get their minds united in a common cause, or feeling, or appreciation. Then the leader will word the prayer so that it can be prayed by the group. Evaluate the following prayers for a group of four- and five-year-olds:

1. "Dear God, we're glad for this beautiful day. Thank You for making the trees and birds and flowers, the blue sky and the warm sunshine. We thank You for our fathers and mothers, our brothers and sisters, our friends and loving relatives. Thank You for the missionaries who are telling people about Jesus. Thank You for our pastor who tells the people in our church what the Bible says. Thank You that we have this Sunday School where we can praise You. In Jesus name, Amen."

2. "Dear Father above, we lift our hearts in praise to Thee for Thy bounteous goodness and tender mercy."

3. "Dear Lord, the boys and girls want to praise You today for your kindness to them. You've given them mothers and fathers and food and homes."

4. (Repeat after the leader.) "Dear Father in heaven, . . .

we praise You . . . for what You have . . . given us today . . . .
We want to . . . love You more . . . each day."

Evaluation (assuming there has been preparation of thought for each prayer):

1. Yes, in evaluating No. 1, you undoubtedly said it's many prayers rather than one. The subjects and the vocabulary are fine for the age-level, but it would be better to have several prayers, each on one subject.

2. The length is fine, but the vocabulary is not at four- and five-year level.

3. This is "about" the children, not "with" them. If they are to pray with the leader, he must word a prayer they can pray. In leading other people we always need to voice what they can make their own prayer.

4. The phrases are short, but so short that the child could not pray intelligibly. Each phrase needs to be a complete or understandable part. Thus it might be: "Dear Father in heaven, . . . thank You for Your good gifts . . . . We love You . . . . We want to love You more."

Thee, Thou?

If we are concerned about making prayer real communion with God we shall not want to use a foreign language, even in part. And the Old English *Thee* is foreign to most small children. Although they may have been in a Christian atmosphere where it is often heard, it does not belong to their mode of expression. They don't voice their own feelings that way. So the answer for most people is, "No, we won't use those words."

However, as the child grows older, some people may feel there is reason to learn this language. If the local church and the home use the King James Bible and hymns using *Thee* and *Thou,* the child will need to become familiar with them. "But," argue some people, "even then they don't need to use them in praying."

If they *are* to learn them, the teaching should wait until school years, and then be gradually and carefully taught, even if the child does hear the terms from others before this. A child can adopt the terminology then with understanding.

Prayer to Whom?
In Scripture there is only one instance where prayer was addressed to Jesus. Stephen as he was being stoned saw the Lord Jesus and prayed, "Lord Jesus, receive my spirit!" (Acts 7: 59) Trinitarian theology tells us that we pray to the Father through the Son by the Spirit.

Because the Lord Jesus is easier for children to comprehend, being now invisible yet in bodily form, many adults lead children in praying to Him. And, of course, He is God so this is not wrong. But some small children have grown to conceive of Jesus as the One who loves little children, and God as the One who punishes evil. This is a dreadful mistake. Let's be sure the children love both God and His Son Jesus. God the Father sent us Jesus because He loved us. Prayers addressed to Jesus should gradually become prayers to God the Father through Christ.

The Lord's Prayer
The prayer Jesus taught His disciples is an example in point. The Christian world will probably long continue to use it with its ancient "art, Thy, Thine," because most people have so learned it, and Christians enjoy praying it together. It would seem wise for children to study it as soon as they are able to appreciate its ideas, so that they can join in this prayer with adults. It is too difficult for most preschoolers.

It is not an easy prayer to teach to children. Sometimes Christian bookstores have materials with which to teach it, in flannelgraph or book form. A family could well take some time to study it phrase by phrase, not all at once. They might center one day's worship around each phrase, illustrating it and praying it.

Said one young person, "I always prayed 'Our Father recharged in heaven.'" Another commented, "I didn't understand 'Thy will be done'—with what?" And several other adults chimed in, "Yes! I always wondered that too."

Children in Prayer Meetings

Rhoda was there . . . but we don't really know how old she was, 8 or 18? Startled at the presence of Peter at the gate, even an adult might have done what she did (Acts 12:13-16). But perhaps Rhoda was only the doorkeeper and not really participating in the prayers of the adults. However, she could have understood and prayed even if she was very small. For the matter for prayer was real and urgent and concrete in nature! Peter was in prison and about to be executed.

And this defines the content for a children's prayer meeting. They can pray about what is real to them. They can pray about what is of current concern to them. They can pray about what is concrete in nature.

If parents wish to bring children under 12 years of age to prayer meeting, it would surely be wise to have them gather in their own groups, perhaps a preschool group and a school-age group. Wise and interested personnel are the chief consideration. Wise in letting the children voice their own concerns and praises, wise in guidance so the prayers are balanced in content (see "What to Pray," p. 75) and varied in form.

Very small children can hold an object, or a picture (clipped from a magazine or drawn to *their* satisfaction) to help them concentrate on their subject for praise. Older children can have their horizons enlarged in terms of God's working in many places in the world.

Since we are thinking about the area of worship rather than petition, we call attention to the need to keep petition from assuming too large a place in the prayer meeting. Yet praise can become monotonous repetition if the children thoughtlessly repeat the same words each time they meet. The leader will need to enlarge the horizons of even the smallest ones to avoid this, though very young children can enjoy repetition to a large extent, especially with a whole week between meetings.

"Prayer meeting" should be a happy thought for children. They will not pray as long a time as the adults, and they may engage in service projects related to answering their prayers.

But they can learn and experience much that will help them to grow toward the life-style God wants—praying without ceasing.

Teaching Children to Lead in Prayer

The best way to teach a child to pray aloud is to help him begin so early that he can't remember having to learn. A tiny child can easily voice a few words of thanks to God. As he grows, his prayers can grow with him. But not automatically. He may need suggestions. Is he praying loud enough for all to hear so that they can pray with him? Does he increasingly think of what all in the group want to pray rather than his own private concerns?

At school age, does he both praise and ask in proportion? Are his prayers increasingly scriptural? Does he word them carefully so others can follow his thought? In the family circle, instruction in prayer can proceed bit by bit without special emphasis.

But in the church group, some children have never learned to pray aloud. Their parents don't pray with them. Again, by starting with nursery children, prayer can be made easy and natural. We talk to God as we talk to each other. The four- and five-year-old can absorb much teaching about prayer, with Bible stories and verses and experience in praying.

In a pre-primary church group, the teachers made a chart to check up on the children's abilities and growth in leading in prayer. The teachers checked after a child's name when he offered to pray aloud, or say the grace for the snack time. They also checked whether he prayed loud enough for all to hear. If not, the leader would say kindly, "We wanted to pray with you, but we couldn't hear what you said to God. Would you like to have me pray with you so everybody can pray?" Before that child led in prayer again, the teacher would suggest, "Will you pray in a loud enough voice so we can all pray with you?"

No child was discouraged by this gentle approach. All learned to lead in prayer. If a child didn't volunteer, a teacher would say, "Maybe you could help us all pray today, Jamie. Let's think what you could say." By helping the child word a prayer, a shy child could be given security. Or the teacher would offer to pray with him the first time. It's very easy to let a few vocal children do all the leading, if leaders aren't aware.

Children between six and eight years can begin by voicing a specific prayer request. The teacher may help a child word his prayer before he prays, and then help him again if he falters, so that the experience is successful and pleasant.

When boys and girls are 9 to 11, they will prefer to begin, if they are unused to praying aloud, in a small group where they are not made conspicuous. Each child in a Sunday School class could decide on one thing to praise God for, and then each pray. If the inexperienced child's turn does not come till several have prayed, he will have a pattern that will make it easy for him to voice his praise.

If we want it to be a pleasant experience, we will not call on a child to pray before the group without asking him ahead of time—unless we are very sure of his willingness.

"I was the preacher's daughter," one woman recalled, "so our Sunday School superintendent assumed I could lead in prayer. I could—I knew all the pious clichés—but I had just reached the point where I realized I was not saved, and I was most unwilling to pray aloud. He pushed me until I did, but it stands out in my mind as a very unhappy experience."

"We all loved our fifth-grade teacher," a student stated. "She prayed so naturally that it seemed easy for us to pray too, the way she did."

9

The Offering as Part of Worship

How Important Is It?

Someone has said that one-fourth of the New Testament deals with stewardship in some form, and that one-third of the words of Jesus deal with the subject! It's impressive to meditate for a moment on the many parables He told in this area, as well as direct teaching. We are first to love God. How is this expressed? We are next to love our neighbor as ourselves. How is this expressed? "Let us not love with word [only]" (1 John 3:18). What astounding things could happen if all Christians were to give even the minimum tithe to God's work!

Sacrificial giving is not easy at first; it needs to begin early in life. The blessedness of giving comes through experience, not by talking about it.

With Preschoolers

Two major questions face us regarding preschoolers with money in their hands: (1) Can they wait till a planned "worship" time to deposit it? (2) Are they really giving when they only transfer money from Father's hand to the receptacle at church?

Most leaders want the children to deposit the money as they

enter, lest they drop it, swallow it, or put it in their ear! And the receptacle has be a closed one, with a hole large enough for undeveloped muscles to get the money in easily. It should be unbreakable, and make a jingling noise. Then at the proper time, it can be brought before the group and the money made a part of worship.

The leader will not say "We give our money to Jesus." To the small child, "to Jesus" means literally to Jesus in person. And the danger exists in his seeing some person, perhaps the Sunday School secretary, pick up the money. Strange ideas have been thus engendered!

The whole idea of giving is nebulous unless the child knows what the money will buy. So we give the money for such practical uses as buying Bibles, paying for the lights and the heat in our church, and buying plane fares for missionaries. Where then does the worship come in? In the *why* of giving. We give *because* we love God and want our money to help in His work.

But is a child really giving? Probably often he is not, for he has no alternative, even after he begins to realize that money will also buy candy. It is the task of both home and church to try to have the child feel it is his money and to have him give it gladly.

A child has to learn the feeling of possession ("It's mine!") before he can release to another. Real giving cannot be forced. So we proceed step by step in such training as a child is able.

Parents can let their child know that as a part of the family, he is sharing in its giving. Such teaching will enlarge as the child grows, encompassing all the areas of stewardship. He will see his parents as models, particularly in their attitude.

Real giving may be better accomplished in a small child's experience if he can give objects that are of value to him, as well as money. Toys for children who do not have any can be collected occasionally with the cooperation of the parents. It is essential that adults be given the role of guidance in the child's selection of what toy he will bring. No broken toy or one the child doesn't like will be a real gift to show Jesus our love. Clothing which has been outgrown, but not outworn, may seem to the small child a very part of himself, and thus become a real gift.

With School Age Children

Primaries and juniors will enjoy having badges or an artificial flower for the ushers to wear. They can learn the correct way to pass the offering plates down the rows and collect them and bring them to the leader for a dedicatory prayer.

Children enjoy having church envelopes like the adults. And the money is thereby less likely to be lost. A family can make these from used paper, or a church can purchase a set of children's envelopes for each child.

Older children will continue to need help in being motivated to give, especially as money becomes more valuable to them. There is so much Scripture on the subject of stewardship that many different verses or stories can be associated with the offering. However, we must remember that in this area too, active listening is not produced merely by saying, "The Bible says," and proceeding to read Scripture. We need to preface a verse with a question or example from everyday life to direct their listening.

"You know that 'poverty' means being poor. What should a group of Christians do when they are going through hard times? Is that not a time to cut down on giving? Many seem to think so. The Macedonians did something different." Then read 2 Corinthians 8:1–3 (in *The Living Bible* for clearest understanding by children). "Let's remember these Christians as we give today."

The next Sunday you could refer to the passage read previously and add, "But they gave something before they gave their money. And it's something the Lord wants us to give first too. And we can if we want to." Read 2 Corinthians 8:1–5.

Or, "Have you experienced the truth of this verse? Jesus said it, so it must be true. 'It is more blessed to give than to receive' (Acts 20:35). Will you give gladly today?"

Older children can sometimes earn money as a special offering to show the Lord their love, such as by raking leaves in the fall, or shoveling snow in the winter, or weeding gardens in the summer.

But for the older children, too, behavior or action can be gifts to the Lord. After appropriate preparation, the children can write out what they are going to do for the Lord during the coming week to show Him their love, and place the paper in the offering receptacle.

One junior group planning to honor God as King discussed what they could do during the week to please Him as a gift. Then when they held the service the next week, they wrote out what they had done and put the slip in the offering plates as a gift already given. The offering receptacle in this casse had been prepared by a group of boys. They cut down a plastic container and wrapped around it a crown they had made and decorated. Several such receptacles could easily be prepared for a large group.

Family projects make excellent outlets for giving, such as taking to the beach, or on a picnic, another family who does not have a car, or pooling savings and earnings to support an orphan overseas. In the context of offering this service to God in love, it becomes a part of worship.

10

Silence in Worship

The world is too much with us. Even in the privacy of our homes the TV and radio fill the air with noise. Crowded housing, sirens, planes, traffic, more and more people—where is the quiet our souls need for worship?

"Be still and know that I am God." "The still small voice." Moses' 40 years in the desert. Paul, also years in the desert. Where is the silence to hear God speak? Is it any wonder our Christian experience often lacks depth? That we do not pray with assurance of God's will? That we wonder too frequently if He really is with us?

Silence can be cultivated, both at home and in a group. Parents can consciously endeavor to have a quiet home, ruling out upsetting topics at meals, or a constantly running TV or radio. A parent can sit down on the bed with a child who has been tucked in, turn out the lights, and suggest something beautiful or wonderful or delightful to think about in silence for a moment or two. Often what fits these superlative adjectives will be about God and His works. Perhaps His starry heaven can be seen out the window. Or flashing lightning. Parent and child can think of all the good things that happened during the day.

Young children in church may listen for sounds: the wind

outside, footsteps going by the door, sounds made by the teacher. They can whisper a prayer to God.

After the story, the teacher may hold up the picture of the story, and let the children look as long as they will in silence. Or she can show a picture and suggest the children try to imagine they are the exemplary character, and how they feel. Pause for them to feel it as long as possible. Watch for such quiet moments and extend them whenever you can so the whole session is not one of constant talking by the teachers. Let the children feel God's presence.

In a worship service praising God for giving us lovely things, a primary group was asked to thank God silently for anything in a picture for which the children were thankful. Then a succession of pictures of lovely things were held up. There were some long moments of attentive silence and probably prayer.

School age children can learn about the Quakers, and experiment with worshiping God in quietness. Soft music can be played, using songs the children know so that their thoughts have direction. For juniors, questions on a flip chart may direct their thinking for some quiet moments. They can meditate on Scripture verses which have words and thoughts within their comprehension without teacher explanation. They can sit quietly and read a simple poem that is worshipful—perhaps taken from a hymn.

Let's not omit quietness in our worship. God may become very near and real in such moments.

11

Art in Worship

The Bible drenches worship in color. The Book of Revelation speaks of a rainbow and coruscating light effects; audio colors include harps and choirs and there are mirror pools and incense. The psalter tells of emotional colors like joy and gladness. Paint worship bright. . . .

It's too bad that piety is often rejected in favor of ascetic regulations which have the appearance of wisdom in promoting rigor of devotion, but are of no value in checking the indulgence of the flesh (Col. 2:23). Bare or gloomy churches are not therefore holy churches, as if the colorless and offensive were stimuli to godliness. While it is possible to go the opposite route and spend millions on plush churches, it is still a fact of Scripture that gladness and color characterize heavenly worship (Paul Fromer, His *magazine, June 1971).*

Have many evangelical Christians in the past overlooked the part of the emotions in worship? Has the worship service tended to be a stiff, staid pattern? Do people ever laugh or cry or sigh or show any emotion? And if such emotions are felt, would they be appropriate to share with other Christians? This may be a matter of disagreement. Some would keep all expression inward. How then can love for each other actually operate?

One point is clear: worship demands feeling. Since art appeals to the emotions, and is a means of expressing them, it can become a means of worship, an aid. The good picture which hangs on the wall of a home for children to see daily creates a certain atmosphere, and unconsciously influences that child. The child can also receive a measure of vicarious expression through it. He gains even more if the picture is discussed by his parents.

Children's Own Expression

The active child is even better served by making his own art express his appreciations and feelings. Adult guidance, wisely given, can utilize this activity to lead to worshiping and expressing appreciation to God. And it can be an individual expression, not a mass response, which so often is not true for all.

In preparation for an Easter worship service, a group of

juniors made a mural on wide shelf paper which went all around a large room when it was put together. Each group concentrated on one day in the last week of the Lord's life on earth, and drew a picture of His activity. Then the parts were fastened to the wall with masking tape, and the whole group walked around the room, stopping by each part. The group which had prepared it explained briefly what they had depicted, then invited the children to sing an appropriate praise song with them, or led the group in prayer, or gave them Bible verses that applied the picture to life. It was a serious, worshipful walk.

Banners can also be valuable to focus thought for primaries or juniors. One group made a banner for each worship service, using no more than two or three words in its design to highlight the focus of the service.

In solemn silence the children hung this banner in front of the group at the beginning of the service. The collected ban-

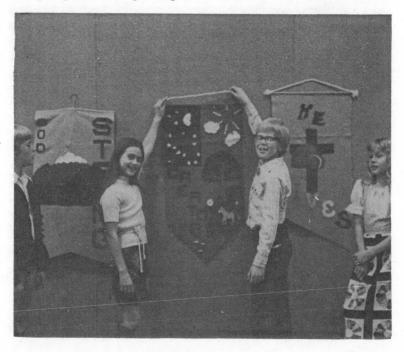

ners were a delightful help at the end of the year in recalling memories of what the group had experienced.

In addition to drawing pictures with crayons, children can enjoy the variety of chalk, painting, cut paper, torn paper, spatter painting, spray painting, collages, mobiles, and every sort of artistic expression. They can be led to use artistic media to express feelings abstractly, as well as to picture concrete things.

A leader may describe a beautiful fun-filled day in the life of a child, and then ask the children to use crayon or paint to show how they might feel at the end of that day. Or describe a quiet time of prayer, and ask them to show the lovely feeling that God was there and they talked with him. They can finger-paint the storm on the Sea af Galilee, with high waves (to music) to get the feel and force of the storm, and then at the end the completely horizontal smooth feeling of peace when Jesus calmed the waves.

To show that God is the giver of joy, a group of primary children each selected a picture of something that made them happy, and then in the worship service, one by one, they placed the pictures on a long strip of brown paper placed across the front of the room, to form a mural of happy things.

For the front of their worship books, juniors studied the meaning of some of the symbols found in the church, such as the cross, a round ball meaning the whole world, and the fish shape used by the early Christians. Then they cut out some symbols or combination of symbols for their covers. They spatter-printed the cover, and then lifted off the symbol to leave a silhouette.

The possibilities of using art are endless. The danger lies in losing the worship emphasis, and enjoying the handwork for itself—in letting it become an end instead of a means. Leaders have the responsibility of maintaining the purpose in the children's minds, and utilizing art to exalt God.

Using Great Art

Since much great art deals with biblical themes, we can use it to lead to worship also. But only if we select pictures carefully in terms of our children, and only if we study the pictures with them. Preschoolers may not be ready for the great differences in culture between their lives and those shown in the paintings. But school age children can profit from thoughtful widening of their appreciation.

For instance, in a medieval painting of a madonna with the Baby Jesus in her lap, the Child does not look at all like a real baby, for His body has the proportions of an adult. This makes Him look peculiar to us. Can the children discover why the Baby looks so strange? Let them look at a picture of a real baby to make comparisons. Babies have large heads and smaller bodies. Did the artist not know this? Or did he intend to say something to us about Jesus?

What could he be saying? Yes, that Jesus, though a baby, was not like other babies, for He had God's wisdom. He was both a baby and God's Son. Of course He actually was shaped

like other babies. But it is a very difficult thought for our minds, that a person could be both God and man. Jesus *was,* the artist is saying. Why is that important to you and to me? Yes, Jesus understands what it's like to be a person. And yes, none but a perfect Person could take the punishment for our sins, could rise from the dead, to be our Saviour. Let's praise Him for being both God and man.

Hoffman's "Boy Jesus in the Temple" hasn't enough action to appeal to young children, but juniors could try to imagine what questions He is asking, study the expressions of the men and suggest what they may be thinking. This could result in praise that Jesus was a boy who asked questions, that we can study the same Bible He had, that children can know truths of God's Word, and so forth.

Another stimulating use of art is to hang before the group two or three pictures of the same event, done by different artists in different ways, and compare them. We can first of all search the Scriptures to see if they are accurate. Then we can try to ascertain whether all the painters are saying the same thing. We can worship God for the truth which means most to us.

Individual pieces of art, including sculpture, will each have their own message. Many can lead to worship if the leader provides guidance in interpreting their message.

Rodin's "The Thinker" may suggest problems people think hard about. "This man could be thinking hard about God. God is so great that men have always done deep, serious thinking about Him. What is the biggest thought or problem in thinking about God that you have?"

Such a question can give you needed insights into the children's understanding of God, and lead to valuable interpretations and answers. "The thought of how God can be everywhere is too great for our minds, but let's sit and think about what that means to us today, and praise Him that it's true even though we can't understand it. How glad we are that God is not as small and limited as we are! We need a great God, one that's too large for our small minds!"

12

Stories and Poetry in Worship

Since worship involves the heart, the feelings, and the will, as well as the intellect, stories and poetry are apt tools. A story can stir feelings and provide a climax in worship, as well as making truth concrete and understandable to children.

Good children's stories for worship are not easy to find. One needs to collect carefully over a period of time. However, if a teacher or parent follows basic storytelling techniques, he may well make up his own which will be suited to the age of the child and the subject of worship. With a little guidance and practice, the children can learn to make up stories. Keep before adult or child the question: Does the story make us admire God and want to praise Him?

Of course Bible story books can provide Bible stories at the children's level. A major caution in using a story is to let the story carry its own moral; let the children tell what it says to us for our lives. If they apply the story, the adult will be kept from "preaching" what is already clear in the story.

Children's songs may be used as poetry as well as music. Children's books of poetry may also serve as worship aids if the adult introduces or follows up the poem with reference to what it indicates or suggests about God, though He may not be mentioned.

With encouragement some children can write delightful poetry. A poem may be a fitting expression of feeling after God has been presented in some aspect of His wonderful nature or activity. In a family, after a happy experience, each one might express how he feeels about God. And there should be no judgment at this time as to literary quality. The poetry may be very free expression.

Some junior girls, who had learned how to write a haiku * in school, enjoyed writing such poems about God in church. The worship focus was on God's wisdom, and they were thinking of His wisdom in making our bodies. Simple poems, but theirs:

> Thank You for my sight.
> I see all things great and small.
> Lord, Your wisdom's great.

> Thank You for my ears.
> Your commands I love to hear.
> Lord, Your wisdom's great.

> You made my body
> With all its little details.
> Lord, Your wisdom's great.

---

* A haiku is an unrhymed Japanese verse form of three lines, containing five, seven, and five syllables respectively, for a total of 17.

13
Movement and Drama in Worship

People who hesitate to use movement and drama in worship with adults often see value in using these with lively, concrete-minded children. Tiny children can be flowers growing out of the ground, feeling praise to God for making them so lovely. They can be birds singing praises to God, the wind blowing, a stream bubbling over rocks, raindrops falling, or leaves whirling.

Praise God for making "me" can be felt vividly as a child jumps, hops, and skips. By contrast, quiet movement and kneeling in prayer, or lifting hands upward, may help a child worship.

Pantomining activities we can do to please God because we love Him can be associated with worship, growing out of it, or leading into it. Hands, feet, eyes, and mind can all help other people in heartfelt gratitude to God for His goodness and helpfulness.

Older children enjoy skits which illustrate truths associated with the worship theme. A primary group decided that one way God was strong was to help them confess and make restitution when they had done wrong. A story about some girls who stole some pencils from the store was left unfinished by the leader. The girls who dramatized the story, and wrote their own ending, impressed the group with the fact that God was strong to help them do what was right even though it was hard to do. Praise to God flowed easily from the dramatization.

At Easter, the reality of the Resurrection was impressive when a junior group took the parts of several Christians gathered a year after the resurrection to recall what they had seen and heard and felt on that great day. Head scarfs for the girls made this scene more realistic.

As they went toward the garden, the women told of their surprise and shock at finding the angel there, and how they ran to tell the disciples. Peter and John recounted how they went to the tomb. And then several recalled how the Lord had come right through the closed door that evening and what He had said and done. The group concluded with a joint enthusiastic statement, "Christ is risen indeed!"

Everyone was then in the mood to sing Easter praises. Such a dramatization can be even more impressive if the adult leaders do it, though usually it's better to have the children putting themselves into the parts. Adults could give a more finished, realistic presentation, and this, too, gives variety.

In a service on God as Judge, a very moving dramatization was done by two boys. One was the judge, dressed in a black robe, with a gavel. The other boy stood before him as the defendant. The judge began reading off a long list of sins which the boy had done (such as, "You have lied" / "You have disobeyed your parents" / "You have been unloving to your sister" / etc.), asking after each one, "Guilty or not guilty?"

The defendant quickly answered "guilty" for some of the charges; at others he hesitated before replying; at a couple he tried to defend himself by such remarks as, "But no worse than anyone else in this courtroom." The judge persisted till the defendant admitted guilt for each. The guilty boy hung his head lower and lower, finally falling on his knees with his head in his hands.

Then the judge asked, "Is there any reason why this boy should not be punished for all these sins he has admitted?"

Whereupon the defendant rose to his feet, stood straight, and said in a clear voice, "Jesus in His own body bore my sins on the cross so that I would not have to be punished for them. I claim Him as my Saviour."

The judge lowered his raised gavel and said, "Case dismissed."

If two juniors cannot be found who can do this with sufficient drama to make it powerful, again, teachers can do it. It makes a great introduction to praising God to show children that while He is a fair and stern Judge, He is also capable of the greatest love and mercy in putting such a punishment on His Son for us.

14
Building a Service for School Age Children (Church Time)

Step 1: Get a Focus

Why are we going to worship God? For what? The children can help in selecting this focus if they are given a list of possibilities, or a number of ideas from which to choose.

Step 2: Think of Ideas to Lead Others to Worship

How can we get other boys and girls to feel like praising God because He is so wonderful in this way we've selected? What will make them marvel at Him? How does this characteristic show?

Experience seems to indicate that most of the varied and interesting ideas will come from adults. But if they are good ideas, the children will quickly take them up and make them their own. The leader will not say, "We're going to do. . . ." Rather, "Let's . . ." / "We can help them praise God if we . . ." / "Wouldn't it be interesting to think of God by . . . ?" / "How would you like to . . . ?" / "What would happen if we . . . ?" / "How could we . . . ?"

In most services we shall plan to use at least the basic elements of worship: the Bible, prayer, and music. Let's brainstorm about the various elements among the concerned leaders:

The Bible   Where does the Bible speak of this characteristic of God? Where is it demonstrated in lives? A concordance leads us to verses, and a cross-reference Bible may assist us. Can we find one verse that is a key or theme verse? What do the verses suggest to us for activities? How can the idea be made real and vivid?

Music   Do our children know any songs on this subject? Are all the stanzas of a hymn on the subject understandable—or too full of symbolism and difficult ideas? Can we select one stanza? Or adapt one? Can we reword that difficult line? Are there any folk songs in this area? Have we consulted the subject index in the hymnbook? Can we write our own stanza? Or set a Bible verse to music?

Offering   Does the focus suggest any special way the children can give their offering? Or a special container? The time will have to be fitted into the service where it is most appropriate and expressive.

Visuals   What can the children do to make the theme concrete? Drama or skit? Their art or great art? Story or poem? Any medium that will create awe and wonder for God, or clarify ideas, highlight points made, establish the mood?

Prayer   When may we expect the group to be ready to express praise and wonder? Leave several possible places, not praying unless the children are ready, but praying when they are. How can the form of prayer be varied? Silent prayer is valuable in involving every person. Conversational prayer can be enjoyable to children. Let's go through the list of possible forms to see which one will fit into this service best.

Readiness for prayer is essential. A sensitive leader will watch for such moments, and not try to have prayer when most of the group are not in the right mood. Occasionally an individual may be asked to remain quiet so that those who wish to pray may do so. God can hardly be expected to want a forced prayer.

Call to worship and benediction   The group may wish to use a call to worship, or a song such as, "Let Us Worship, Singing."

Children can learn a group call to worship, or an individual may be chosen by his peers to give the call, standing quietly in front of them till all are ready to hear it. We may wish to select one of the following verses or passages:

Psalm 95:1–3, 6	Psalm 100	Psalm 103:1
Psalm 105:1–3	Psalm 105:4	Psalm 34:3
Psalm 46:10a	Isaiah 25:1	Isaiah 55:6
James 4:8a		

A benediction may be chosen from a group of verses, and given in various ways. It may be sung by the whole group, hummed as one person sings it, played on an instrument by a child or teacher, or be a whispered dismissal when everyone is quiet enough to hear it. After a service on God as Peace, the leader dismisses the group by saying softly, "Go in peace." The following verses may be used.

2 Corinthians 13:14	Numbers 6:24–26
Philippians 4:23	Jude 24–25
Hebrews 13:20–21	

Step 3: Organize the Parts.

What will be the climax of the service? Where can we expect most reverence if we've set the climate for it? Let's arrange the parts in psychological order, to lead the group step by step in praise and adoration. Vary the kinds of activity and intersperse songs, standing and sitting, and prayer.

Step 4: Have the Children Prepare.

The groups of children will each prepare their part of the service, both rehearsing it, and praying for its use by God. The whole group will come together to learn a new song, for we don't want to "teach" in the worship service. Those in charge of the new song will display the words in large letters on a sheet of newsprint in front of the group, and ask questions about the words to get the children to understand the meaning of the song. Call attention to some idea in the song before it is sung several times, perhaps first by the teachers, then played on a record, and finally sung by the teaching group of children. Perhaps the teaching group have made pictures to help explain the song. (See "Teaching a Song" in chap. 7.)

Another group may wish to teach everyone a response to the call to worship, or to explain what to do during the reading of the benediction. Preparations are made now so that the service can be truly expressive, and not so new and unfamiliar the children cannot think about God. Also a spirit of anticipation is thereby raised. There will be enough that is different, since each group does not know how the others are going to do their parts. An experienced children's educator reports:

"We found participation by the children costly in terms of time. They could not prepare their parts well enough to put on a truly worshipful service the same Sunday, since we only had an hour and a half in which to do it. So we spent one week preparing, and doing some handwork on their worship books. The next week we had the service, and then made a memory page about the service for their books, or some similar project.

"We could not expect even juniors who had been to Sunday School for an hour to continue in serious thought all during church time. They needed a change of pace and activity each week.

"But though we were a bit embarrassed at first to admit that the children did not have a worship service every week, we soon lost that feeling. The preparation week was valuable, as they were working to get others to feel worshipful toward God. They were involved in thinking about God! In our preparation hour, we had to motivate them to appreciate the aspect of God upon which we were building the service, so it had its moments of worship too, even though we didn't label it as worship. And they were mastering materials devoted to God's praise."

Step 5: An Adult Coordinates the Session

A teacher will need to take responsibility for putting all the parts of the service together so that the service flows, and is not a disjointed collection of bits and pieces. This leader carefully plans meaningful transitions, or asks the group to introduce its part to accomplish this purpose.

Transitions are not "Now we'll sing No. 54" or "Now bow your heads for prayer." They concern the content, helping the group keep the theme in view, and the purpose of the next part of the service. "This song will help us think of some of the ways God never changes." And after the song, the leader may comment, "What a wonderful God! Let's tell Him how glad we are that He never changes. Let's each do it silently."

Step 6: Prepare to Worship.

If the preparation discussed in chapter 3 has been thoroughly understood by the children, it will only now and then have to be reviewed in detail. Instead, a quiet invitation to have a moment of silence to get ready for worship will remind them. For a new child the group will explain what they do to prepare, thus reviewing and assuring the leader they do remember what the moment of silence should accomplish.

Step 7: Worship in the Service.

If possible, have the worship service in a special room not used by the groups or for the preparation period. This is often possible during church when so many Sunday School rooms are not in use. If not, it still may be wise to send the children to their group gathering place, from where they may come in silence to the worship service.

As they come, a prelude may be played by a child who is able, or by a teacher, or by using a tape or record. If from the first adults set a pattern of silence, the opening of the service can be impressive.

When the group has all gathered, one child carries the banner to the front, or the picture, or the word which highlights the focus of the service, and places it before the group. And the service proceeds in a dignified, yet informal manner. The Holy Spirit then has a situation He can use to speak to hearts, through an orderly and progressive series of thoughts and activities which the children understand. There will be responses from the group, child-like participation in testimonies and illustrations, and hence freedom for the Spirit even though the service has been carefully planned.

The leaders will see themselves as fellow-worshipers with the children, not merely onlookers. They will give a testimony when it is appropriate as they would in an adult gathering, and they will sing and pray sincerely. Hypocrisy on their part will be easily discerned by the children. And if all this is "only for children," it will not be very impressive to the children, no matter how much work has gone into it. Leaders need to be able to talk easily about their feelings toward God, to show their awe and reverence, to be "with" the group, not "over" it.

In dealing with the subject of prayer, one group told the others of God's three answers to prayer: yes, no, and wait. They had constructed a stoplight to show the three answers (green—yes; red—no; yellow—wait). They gave a puppet show illustrating how Corrie Ten Boom had received these three answers.

Then the junior leaders asked if any of the children could give an illustration of a time when they'd had a yes, no, or wait answer from God. There was immediate response in each area. Both teachers and children shared experiences. Later the whole group evaluated this part of the service as one of the highlights.

The younger the group, the more informality and movement needs to be expected and planned. Preschoolers will not plan and prepare, but must be involved if it is to be real to them. Their service will be shorter, or broken up by some physical movement.

Primaries are at mid-way point. They can do some planning and preparation, but the bulk of the service will probably be carried by the adult leaders. It takes longer for this age to get ready to lead the group effectively, than for older children.

Step 8: Evaluate
After the postlude has been played, or the benediction given,

or the group dismissed to their small groups, a casual evaluation will be helpful to the leaders. Some of the following questions may be asked—not all at once:

- Were you ready to meet God today?
- Did you really meet God today?
- Did you really praise Him?
- Did you really speak to Him?
- Did He really speak to you?
- What helped you most to worship (if you did)?
- Which part do you think pleased God most?
- Was there anything that kept you from worshiping God?

Discussing the service with the children will help leaders know how to shape future services to bring God close, and keep them from thinking quiet children are necessarily worshiping.

If leaders work and pray, and expect spiritual results in lives, God will not disappoint them. He seeks people to worship Him in spirit and in truth. Even though we cannot expect to see all that occurs within a child, we can ask the Lord for enough evidence to encourage us that His Spirit is working. Our part is to be sure we are working with Him, not violating His established process of development.

15

Worship Services Illustrated

A Worship Service with Juniors

Picture a group of 25-30 nine- to eleven-year-olds, all of whom have professed salvation. They come largely from church families, and attend regularly. They are divided into three groups of boys and three groups of girls with men as leaders for boys, and women for the girls. The attendance varies so that one group has eight and one has two during the session described.

The illustration purposes to show what actually was done, not what *you* can do. Every situation is different, in terms of leaders and children, time and space. You may have 10 primaries and one leader, or 100 children and 10 leaders, or primaries and juniors together with two leaders. Look for the illustration of principles, and then consider how you can use these principles.

Step 1: Our focus—To appreciate that God is omnipotent. We decided to use this word since juniors could understand it, and enjoy learning new large words.

Step 2: Getting ideas—The leaders brainstormed. Where is God's power shown? In nature (juniors are intrigued by the facts and marvels of science), in Bible events, and in men's lives through the work of God.

Where is nature? The microcosm—the atom; the macro-cosm—the heavens. Bible verses about atoms and stars. A mobile of the solar system?

Where in the Bible? Daniel, Peter walking on the water, Israel crossing the Red Sea. Innumerable instances there, many of which the children should be able to suggest. Pictures. Pantomimes for the others to guess? Interviews.

Where is man? Changes in lives through salvation and going God's way. Testimonies? Have our children experienced God's working? Living people? Sports heroes? They've read the comic book version of Corrie Ten Boom's life. Teachers' testimonies?

What songs do we already know that mention God's power? "How Great Thou Art," and we have a picture book of it. And "I Sing the Mighty Power of God," which could be easilly illustrated. Perhaps one group could write a praise response to sing after each illustration of God's power.

The praise response could be real prayer to God. There may be a high moment for it at other places, to be determined by the groups as they work out their parts, or by the leaders.

The offering receptacle could be decorated with nature objects.

Visuals? Each group could place a picture or object related to their part on a large board in front, around the word *omnipotent*.

Step 3: Organizing the parts—We'll begin with nature, and work up to the interior power of God in changing men's lives. That brings it home to each one personally for a climax.

Step 4: Preparing in groups—A group of 6th grade boys made a long mural to show God's omnipotence in the marvels of water. One boy brought his microscope and they all looked at a drop, then drew a large-sized one with living things in it for the mural. They talked about what happens when water freezes—the marvel that it doesn't sink, and made a scene of a frozen lake surface with fish and plants alive underneath. They made water in an irrigation ditch with vegetables growing alongside. The leader showed them how to paint with gluey water over green and blue tissue paper to give their scenes a watery effect. They made a large drop of water to place on the central visual board.

A group of fifth- and sixth-grade girls studied a children's book on the stars. They looked up facts in the encyclopedia at home during the week (with a reminder phone call from their leader), and found references to the stars in the Bible. They eagerly adopted the leader's suggestion for presenting their facts and verses. As they stood in a line before the group the first girl gave a fact or two, the second read a Bible verse, then the group said, "This God is our God." Then the third girl gave a fact, the fourth a verse, the group recited. They made several stars covered with glitter to put on the visual board.

The music group of fifth- and sixth-grade girls illustrated the words of "I Sing the Mighty Power of God," and decided which words needed a bit of clarification for the group. Two went through the picture book of "How Great Thou Art" to practice turning the pages at the right time. Then they worked together to make up first the words, then the music for a brief praise refrain. They discussed teaching this to the whole group, and emphasizing that it was to be each person's own praise to God, not just a song. They made some musical notes to put on the visual board.

The fourth-grade boys decided to interview Bible characters who had experienced God's power. Following the example set by their leader, each one began similarly with great enthusiasm, "Have you seen God's power?" And the boy being interviewed replied, "Have I seen God's power! I'm Daniel, and the king threw me into a den of lions because I prayed. Those lions were hungry, I tell you!" In their own words the boys told what they had felt and experienced. They made an open Bible to place on the visual board.

The fifth-grade boys made a drawing of an atom to place on the visual board, and gave some facts about the construction of matter. They featured Colossians 1:17—that God not only made everything but that He holds it all together.

The leader of a group of girls first gave her testimony as to how God changed her when she became a Christian. She asked the group to think about their own lives. Had God made a difference in their lives? In what way? To her delight each of the five girls responded positively. They told of changes of attitude toward girls they didn't like, of obeying instead of rebelling at home. One told of witnessing to a girl she knew. For the visual board they made two stick figures, with a cross between them. On one side the figure had a bent head and arms at its sides; on the other side of the cross the figure was erect with arms out.

Step 5: Coordinating the service—The leader planned the transitions, or asked each group if they wished to introduce their part, and told each group when they were to participate in the service.

Step 6: Preparing to worship—Since the children were familiar with the steps in getting ready, the leader asked for a quiet moment to get ready.

Step 7: Worshiping—The piano was playing the new praise response as the children came into the worship area.

In impressive silence, a boy placed the letters in the center of the visual board: O M N I P O T E N T .

"We worship an omnipotent God," the leader began. "Let's tell Him how great we know He is." One girl placed the notes on the visual board. Two girls held up the picture book of "How Great Thou Art," the pianist played a short introduction, and the children sang.

The leader of the group which had studied the stars gave the transition to their part. "If we look up into God's heavens, we find out how great He is." The first girl began with the facts about the stars, the next read her Bible verse, and all repeated, "This God is our God," etc.

A girl from the music group held up the large sheet on which the praise response was written. "Let's praise God for the stars," she said. The pianist played a chord, and the group sang the praise response.

"God not only shows His power in the heavens," said the leader of the next group, "but scientists are finding out amazing things about matter, which we cannot see even with the strongest microscopes." The boys gave their facts about the atom, held up a large poster of Colossians 1:17 for the whole group to read together, and placed a drawing of an atom on the board.

Then the girls showed their illustrations of the words of "I Sing the Mighty Power of God" as the pianist played the music. A second time they invited the group to sing as they showed their pictures.

The boys showed their mural about water and explained it. The whole group sang the praise response.

The fourth-grade boys held their interviews with the Bible characters (using the mike from the tape recorder), and again the group sang the praise response.

"But the greatest work of all to show God's power," said the leader of the girl's group, "is what He can do inside us." The girls placed their figures with the cross on the visual board. Then each girl in the group stood and told how God had changed her attitude. And one of the girls concluded, "Has God changed you? Do you want to tell us about it?" Three children responded with earnest stories of what God had done for them in relationships with others.

"This time," said the leader, "as the piano plays the praise response, let's pray it silently, thinking of what God has done for us or wants to do for us."

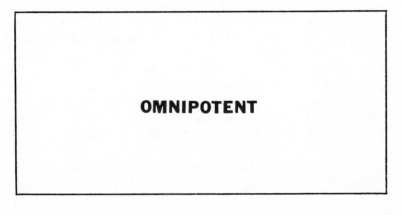

OMNIPOTENT

Then the children were dismissed, group by group, to their meeting places in small groups.

Step 8: Evaluating—The leaders asked the children what part of the service they found most helpful in worshiping God. Many of them were impressed by the testimonies of changes in lives.

The leaders brought up the topic for the next service, and asked for any ideas as to how we could worship God because He is unchanging. Responses were minimal, but prepared the children to accept suggestions the following week.

Each group then made either a sheet for their notebook to remember the service on omnipotence, or a part of their wall hanging, which two girls' groups were making. Most of the groups chose to show something about the part they'd had— which confirms again the importance of participation. They cut outlines of stars, or stick men or an atom, pinned them to a paper on a square of cardboard, and spatter painted them to get a clear silhouette.

A Worship Service with Primaries

Picture a group of 30 six- to eight-year-olds, most of whose parents are in adult church as the children gather for Primary Church. There is one adult leader, and three young people who are apprentices-in-training for a period of six weeks, then to be replaced by three other young people (not an ideal arrangement). The children are divided by grades, with a young person in charge of each grade.

Step 1: Our focus—To obey God by praising Him with instruments as well as with singing.

Step 2: Getting ideas—What means of praise does the Bible mention? The adult leader used a concordance and discovered clapping and many kinds of instruments.

What kinds of instruments could the four leaders collect? They were able to assemble: large nails (one hung by a bright heavy yarn, struck by another nail for a lovely tinkling sound), some toy instruments, some homemade shakers (a number of film cans with a few beans in each), a wooden xylophone (which had a complete scale), an autoharp, a set of tuned glasses (adding water to get the correct scale tones), and a toy drum.

How were we to play? The Bible mentioned melody (Ps. 27:6c) which infers it sounds well, and playing skillfully (Ps. 33:3) which means practice.

The children would enjoy all the instruments, but would it be worship? We would need to think through with them the fact that music with the instruments would be praise only if there were praise inside us as we played. We could show this emphasis from Scripture:

- Colossians 3:16—"with thankfulness in your hearts to God"
- Ephesians 5:19—"making melody with your heart to the Lord"
- 1 Chronicles 15:16—"to raise sounds of joy"
- Psalms 47:1—"voice of joy"

Primaries need to have each part of the program shorter than juniors, with more physical activity and participation. We shall have both preparation and worship service in one session.

Step 3: Organizing the parts—We'll introduce the kinds of praise and how we are to play first, followed by a practice period. Then we can have a procession to come to the worship service. Each group can lead the others in one song, introducing it so everyone praises the Lord inside as the Bible tells us to do. We'd better begin with prayer that our worship will be inside as we play, to get that emphasis in focus.

After the worship service, we can trade instruments in the groups to try them out, if the children would like to do that. Or we could write "Singing and making melody with your heart to the Lord" (Eph. 5:19) in the center of a page (or have it already written for the first graders), and draw pictures of instruments around the verse.

Step 4: Preparing in groups—The first graders used the nails to practice a soft worshipful song, "Holy is the Lord." They decided to introduce it by announcing:

"The Lord is holy—perfectly good.
We are going to praise Him with soft sounds.
You can sing softly to praise Him with us."

The second graders had a variety of toy instruments and shakers. They practiced a marching song for the procession "Enter into His Gates." Their introduction was: "Let's praise the Lord as we march and sing. We can enter into His courts with praise and be thankful to Him." When the children were seated, the second graders would lead the others in clapping and singing "Praise Him."

The third graders had the individual instruments. Two of them worked together on each one, using songs suggested by the leader as easiest to play. Two tried to play "Jesus Loves Me" on the glasses, and two others on the xylophone, and two others on the autoharp. Others used the shakers and planned to distribute them.

Step 5: Coordinating the service—The leader had planned the transitions, or had assigned each group leader the introduction to his group's part.

Step 6: Preparing to worship—The leader played on the piano, "Enter into His Gates," and each group leader got his children lined up ready to march. The first and second graders played as they walked, the others clapped or used shakers. The stationary instruments were set on a table at the front of the room.

Step 7: Worshiping—The children sat down and were asked to place their instruments under their chairs. "Our voices can make the softest music of all," the leader began. "Let's hum softly 'Holy is the Lord' and begin to think about Him."

The worshipful soft songs were sung first to the accompaniment of the nails. The leader introduced each in terms of how we could praise the Lord inside by singing it outside.

Then the second graders played the instruments and led the group in clapping to some of the louder songs.

The third graders had succeeded in working out "Jesus Loves Me" on the xylophone. (They were given the letters which were on the pieces of wood, for the first line, and they wrote down the others as they practiced the song.) But the complete song had not been worked out on the glasses or autoharp. So one child was asked to strike a key note as the piano played the song. A leader played the glasses, with a child hitting a key note, as the leader nodded to him.

As the whole group silently thanked God for the things we'd used in worship, the leader named them and paused for a second or two after each:

- our ears to hear music
- our fingers to play music
- our voices to sing music
- our feet to walk to music
- our hands to clap to music

She concluded: "You made us, dear God, so we could do all these things to praise You. We thank You. You are very great and wonderful. Amen."

Step 8: Evaluating—The leaders quickly listed for their groups all the parts of the worship service, and asked what part they thought God liked best. Most of the children thought He would have liked "Holy Is the Lord" to the accompaniment of the nails. They thought it was hardest to think about God when they were walking and playing too.

For their notebooks, some chose to draw pictures of the toy instruments they had used, but others preferred to look at the real orchestral instruments pictured on the bulletin board, and draw those. Third-graders were encouraged to draw the instruments they might like to learn to play in praise of the Lord.

Results

Can children worship "in spirit and in truth"? Can they focus on God? Can they meet Him through our planning and work? After the junior service described, a fifth-grade girl wrote to a friend: "We had a worship service today in Junior Church. I really felt I talked to God and He talked to me too. It was on how God is omnipotent. Wow, is He smart."

A Checklist

1. **Do I have a clear focus?**
   Is it specific?
   Will it lead each boy and girl to meet God?
   Is worship clearly differentiated in my own mind from instruction about God?

2. **Do the children understand the purpose of the service too?**
   Can they define worship adequately?

3. **Does each part contribute to the over-all purpose?**
   Is it arranged psychologically to lead to a climax?
   Is there variation?
   Sufficient movement? (standing to sing, participation)
   Are there carefully planned transitions between the parts so that the service flows in thought?

4. **Is Primary or Junior Church different from Sunday School?**
   Seating?
   Type of activity?

5. **Is there motivation for participation?**
   Are plans stimulating enough to draw volunteers?
   Do the children aim to help everyone worship?
   Are they involved as much as possible in the planning?

6. **Is everything at the children's level?**
   In vocabulary and concepts?
   In feeling and experience?
   In interest and ability?

7. **Music**
   Is the song introduced in a meaningful context?
   Do the children hear it several times before they sing it?
   Are the words explained where necessary?
   Can the children paraphrase the meaning?
   Are you using the children's talents?
   Do you have a standard for the worship service, encouraging those who do not play well enough to keep practicing?
   Each time a song is sung, do you direct thought to the message so the children think what they're singing?

8. **Scripture**

Are experiences in reading and using Scripture pleasant?

Are verses carefully selected for the children's understanding and needs?

Are those who read Scripture prepared? Do they practice reading?

Do you print verses in large letters for the whole group to read?

Do you discuss and explain hard words?

Before Scripture is read, do you prepare the group to listen *for* something?

9. **Prayer**

Are the children prepared to pray, not in posture, but in thought and feeling, each time they pray?

Are prayers worded from the children's viewpoints, not the adult leader's?

Is the prayer expressive of children's interests and needs?

Does it express their praises?

Can they honestly pray it?

Are all the children learning to lead in prayer?

Is there variety in the forms of prayer?

memorized (Lord's Prayer)

conversational

silent

song

Scripture

teacher

Bible verse addressed to God

litany

composed by the children, and read

Are worship prayers largely praise and adoration?

10. **Do you get the children's viewpoint afterward?**

When did they feel near to God?

What hindered them?

11. **Are you using good group techniques?**

Do you wait for quiet before you begin to talk?

Do you sometimes say an individual's name quietly?

Do you watch the seating to avoid problems?

Do you demand quiet by your poise and manner?

Do leaders sit in strategic places in the group?

Do you plan your major questions, so they require thought?

Do you watch reactions of the whole group? speak to the whole group? get answers from the whole group?

Do you vary your reactions to answers? Do you avoid responding "Good!" for answers requiring no thought as well as those which do? Instead of saying "OK" continually, do you sometimes give a nod of appreciation, or say "Thank you"?

Do you have a flexible plan, timed but adjustable? Can you delete or add according to the responses of the children?

Do you plan the service so the climax will not be interrupted by the ringing of a bell or the end of church?

Do you avoid telling the children what they can tell? Or doing what they can do? (Except occasionally to save time)

Do you make the children's answers important for all to hear by not repeating them? (Sometimes you may ask a child to speak louder so all can hear his correct answer.)

Do you use all possible visual aids?

Do you balance love with firmness so the children can feel the security of someone in control?

Do you avoid asking the children to "tell me" when you know the answers? Or "tell us" because what you really desire is to get the answer before the group? (Why ask if everyone knows?)

12. Is handwork a servant of the message?

Do you carefully consider the purpose of each project, the time it will take, the difficulty it will pose for the age of the child doing it?

Do you give directives before distributing any materials?

Do you demonstrate and explain?

Do you make cleaning up part of the project, to insure the children are also learning responsibility?

Appendix

Characteristics of God from Isaiah

chastens   48:10
comforts   49:13; 51:3, 12; 59:9
compassionate   49:13; 54:10
controls man's life   40:23-24
Creator of heavens and earth   50:26, 28; 41:4; 42:5; 44:24; 45:7, 18; 48:13; 51:13, 16; 54:5
Creator of man   43:1; 51:13
doesn't forget His own   49:14-15
does what He says   44:26-28; 46:11
eternal   57:15
faithful   49:7
first, and with last   41:4
gentle   40:11; 42:3
gives Spirit and blessing   44:3
guides   48:17; 49:10; 58:11
hears   59:1
Helper   41:10, 13, 14, 17, 18, 19, 20; 40:10-11; 29, 31
help to old age   46:4
His Word is forever   40:8
holy   41:14, 16; 43:3, 14-15; 57:15
Judge   41:1, 5, 11; 42:3-4, 24; 43:15
King   43:15; 44:6; 52:7
mighty, strong   40:10, 12, 17, 22-23, 28-30; 41:10, 13; 49:26; 42:13; 43:13, 16; 44:6
of order   45:18-19
only One   45:1-22; 44:6, 8; 45:5-6, 22; 45:18, 21; 46:9; 48:12
pardons   55:7
Redeemer, Saviour   41:14; 44:6, 22; 43:1, 3, 14, 25; 59:20; 45:17, 22
reveals Himself   45:3; 48:16; 51:4, 16
rewards those who wait for Him   49:23
righteous   45:21, 24
salvation forever   51:6, 8
satisfies   58:11
sees us, our way, our right   40:27
shows men who He is   41:20, 26